# 100
## BEST SELLING
## ALBUMS OF THE
# 90s

# 100
## BEST SELLING
## ALBUMS OF THE

# 90s

Peter Dodd    Justin Cawthorne    Chris Barrett    Dan Auty

This 2009 edition published by 3C Publishing Ltd by arrangement with Amber Books Ltd.

3C Publishing Ltd
Sky House
Raans Road
Amersham
Bucks, HP6 6JQ

Editorial and design by:
Amber Books Ltd
Bradley's Close
74–77 White Lion St
London N1 9PF
United Kingdom
www.amberbooks.co.uk

ISBN: 978-1-906842-07-9

Project Editor: Tom Broder
Design: Colin Hawes
Picture Research: Natasha Jones
Consultant: Roger Watson

ACKNOWLEDGEMENTS

Thanks to the following for help with supplying the albums as well as for their invaluable industry knowledge:
Reckless Records (www.reckless.co.uk), Soho, London
Flashback (www.flashback.co.uk), Islington, London
Golden Grooves (www.goldengroovesrecords.com), Old Street, London
Haggle (www.hagglevinyl.com), Islington, London
The Music and Video Exchange, Notting Hill, London
Stage and Screen, Notting Hill, London
Beanos (www.beanos.co.uk)

Printed in China

# Contents

**Editor's introduction** . . . . . . . . . . . . . . . . . . . . . . . . . . . . . . . . . . . . 6

**Introduction** . . . . . . . . . . . . . . . . . . . . . . . . . . . . . . . . . . . . . . . . . . . 8

**Albums** 100–91 . . . . . . . . . . . . . . . . . . . . . . . . . . . . . . . . . . . . . . . . 16
**Albums** 90–81 . . . . . . . . . . . . . . . . . . . . . . . . . . . . . . . . . . . . . . . . . 36
**Albums** 80–71 . . . . . . . . . . . . . . . . . . . . . . . . . . . . . . . . . . . . . . . . . 56
**Albums** 70–61 . . . . . . . . . . . . . . . . . . . . . . . . . . . . . . . . . . . . . . . . . 76
**Albums** 60–51 . . . . . . . . . . . . . . . . . . . . . . . . . . . . . . . . . . . . . . . . . 96
**Albums** 50–41 . . . . . . . . . . . . . . . . . . . . . . . . . . . . . . . . . . . . . . . . 116
**Albums** 40–31 . . . . . . . . . . . . . . . . . . . . . . . . . . . . . . . . . . . . . . . . 136
**Albums** 30–21 . . . . . . . . . . . . . . . . . . . . . . . . . . . . . . . . . . . . . . . . 156
**Albums** 20–11 . . . . . . . . . . . . . . . . . . . . . . . . . . . . . . . . . . . . . . . . 176
**Albums** 10–1 . . . . . . . . . . . . . . . . . . . . . . . . . . . . . . . . . . . . . . . . . 196

**Appendix: Facts and figures** . . . . . . . . . . . . . . . . . . . . . . . . . . . . . 216

**Index** . . . . . . . . . . . . . . . . . . . . . . . . . . . . . . . . . . . . . . . . . . . . . . . 220

# Editor's foreword

The ranking of the 100 best-selling albums of the 1990s listed in the following pages is based upon the number of platinum and multi-platinum sales awards each album has achieved, as certified by the Recording Industry Association of America (RIAA) and the British Phonographic Industry (BPI). The RIAA platinum award represents sales of at least 1,000,000 albums; the BPI platinum represents sales of at least 300,000 albums.

In an industry not always noted for the accuracy of its published sales figures, these awards provide one of the most effective and reliable measures of sales success. Unlike similar lists based on chart position, these figures also show sales from the date of first release right up to the present day. This means an album such as No Doubt's *Tragic Kingdom*, which failed to chart on release in 1995 but has sold well ever since, is rated above an album such as Vanilla Ice's *To The Extreme*, which spent 16 weeks at Number One but could not maintain these sales for any length of time.

### Ranking of equal sellers

Where two or more albums in the list have the same sales total they are arranged by date of release, with the most recent album released ranked highest, since its sales are stronger relative to time spent on the market. The Stone Temple Pilot's 1992 album *Core*, for example, has had almost a decade longer to achieve its sales of 8,100,000 than Christina Aguilera's 1999 self-titled debut album, and is therefore ranked lower in the list.

### Compilations and soundtracks

Compilation or greatest hits albums are not included in this list, although live albums and original movie or musical soundtracks, where all of the songs have been collected together or recorded specifically for the album, are featured. The soundtrack to the 1994 film *Forest Gump*, for example, featured tracks from artists ranging from Elvis and Joan Baez to The Supremes, and helped introduce a whole new generation to classic songs from the preceding decades.

### US and international album sales

Although the lists in this book are based on both US and UK album sales, the sheer size of the North-American album market relative to that of other regions means that the list is inevitably weighted toward US top-sellers. Nonetheless,

British bands are well represented, with albums from artists ranging from Eric Clapton and Oasis to the Spice Girls all making it into the list. The albums are illustrated using a mixture of US and UK sleeve designs – a selection that includes some of the most iconic images of the decade.

**Facts and figures**

The appendices provide a breakdown of some of the most interesting facts and figures found throughout this book. You can find out which artists have the most albums in the list and who are the highest-ranking US and UK acts. You can see which albums have won the most Grammy awards or contain the most Number One singles, what are the best-selling soundtracks and live albums, and which record labels were the most successful of the decade.

Alongside tributes to old favourites there are enough surprises to keep the most dedicated music buff guessing and stimulate plenty of lively discussion. Nirvana's genre-defining 1991 album *Nevermind,* for example, was comfortably outsold by fellow grunge-rockers Pearl Jam's album *Ten*, released just a few month earlier. No less than three albums from country-music superstar Garth Brooks, meanwhile, have outsold *...Baby One More Time,* Britney Spears' highest-ranking album of the decade.

Carlos Santana's 1999 release *Supernatural*, his 28th album in a career spanning four decades, won an astonishing eight Grammy awards, more than any other album featured in the 100 best-selling albums of the 1990s.

# The Best-Selling Albums of the 1990s

In the 1990s, the album charts opened up to encompass a greater variety of sounds and styles than ever before. Grunge bands like Pearl Jam and Nirvana brought guitar rock and a punk aesthetic back into the mainstream. Hip hop finally began to reap the commercial rewards it had promised for so long, silencing those who had dismissed it as a passing fad, and other urban sounds, from R&B to dance, filled the charts. There was room, too, for strong, commercial pop. But it was country music that really dominated the decade, with artists such as Garth Brooks and Shania Twain helping reinvigorate the genre, injecting a healthy dose of sex and style.

The 1990s saw women become market leaders in a way that exceeded even Madonna's 1980s' achievements. Not many people would have bet that the end of the decade would see a female country singer at the top of the best-sellers, triumphantly tossing her cowboy hat in the air. But while Shania Twain led the pack, she was not the only female artist to ride high in the charts. Female solo artists – from Alanis Morissette to Melissa Etheridge – dominated 1990s' music, while girl bands such as TLC and the Spice Girls also gave the boys a good run for their money.

## Fighting the pirates

The early 1990s saw the music industry enjoying a boom period. By 1992 sales of compact discs had outpaced tape cassettes and were growing all the time; the CD's unrivalled sound quality and ease-of-use made them the format of choice for most 1990s music buyers.

But there was a downside to the CD revolution – music pirates were quick to spot the potential for selling counterfeit CDs, adding an element of instability to the economics of the music industry. The Far East proved to be a haven for CD pirates; in the Philippines the situation was so bad it was estimated that half of all CDs sold there were pirate copies. The problem was by no means exclusive to East. In any European or North American city, traders could be found selling their wares on street corners. By the end of the 1990s, it was estimated that over 640,000,000 pirated discs were sold annually.

## Technological advances

Illegal CDs were not the only problem facing the music industry. The creation in 1997 of the MP3 format – a digital file format that allowed audio files to be reduced in size and transmitted over the internet – meant that anyone with an MP3 player or a CD-writer on their computer could download and record music illegally. Several major courtroom battles between record companies and illicit net operators did little to contain the problem, although the full effects of the new technology on the album market would not be felt until after the end of the decade.

The 1990s also saw a growing number of bands embracing the opportunities offered by the internet, by giving concerts on the net or providing fans with the opportunity to legally download music clips. Hootie & The Blowfish, one of the most bizarrely named bands to grace the charts, played an internet concert from Chicago's House Of Blues in October 1998. Their 1994 album *Cracked Rear View* sold over 10,000,000 copies by the winter of 1995, making it Atlantic Records' best seller.

### Established artists

The 1990s' album chart also featured plenty of old timers rubbing shoulders with fresh new talent like Hootie. CDs and the Internet were unheard of when Carlos Santana formed his band Santana in the 1960s. Three decades later, Santana were back at the top of the album chart with *Supernatural*, an album featuring collaborations with a host of 1990s' stars

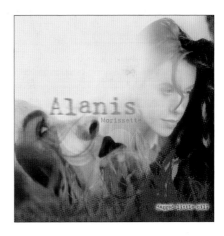

The angst-filled songs on Alanis Morissette's multi-platinum album *Jagged Little Pill* – like the harder, punk-inspired sound of grunge bands such as Nirvana – showed that in the 1990s, 'angry' definitely sold records.

including Lauryn Hill and Eagle Eye Cherry. In December 1996, Santana received a prestigious Century Award from *Billboard* magazine, honoring his contribution to music.

Meat Loaf was another established star to continue to do good business in the 1990s. His gothic rock-opera masterpiece *Bat Out Of Hell* was originally released in 1977, when it had even managed to knock *Saturday Night Fever* off the top of the Australian chart. The sequel, *Bat Out Of Hell II*, was released 16 years later in 1993, when it made the Number One spot on both sides of the Atlantic. Another seasoned performer was Eric Clapton, who did particularly well with *Unplugged*, recorded during his acoustic concert for MTV in January 1992.

### Cowgirls and cowboys

Shania Twain led a growing band of 1990s artists who fused country with pop and rock, taking country music away from its large but middle-aged specialist audience and widening its appeal. Released in November 1997, Twain's mega-selling album *Come On Over* showed the level of this appeal by topping the country and mainstream charts simultaneously. Twain's songwriting and production partner was her husband, the heavy-metal producer, Mutt Lange, who had powered Def Leppard to fame.

Hot on Shania Twain's trail came the Dixie Chicks, three cowgirl divas who crossed barriers with their dramatic album *Wide Open Spaces* to become the best selling country act in 1998. Garth Brooks also rode tall with two albums comfortably nestling against each other high in the 1990s' album chart. Like Shania Twain, Brooks redefined country, producing haunting, mystical songs that soon had other artists lining up to do cover versions. Brooks has sold over 90,000,000 albums – more than even Elvis Presley, according to figures from the Recording Industry Association of America (RIAA).

Even Whitney Houston was influenced by country music in the 1990s. The soundtrack album to the movie *The Bodyguard* featured a revamp of Dolly Parton's country classic 'I Will Always Love You'. Houston's big-production, power-ballad spent a record-breaking 14 weeks at the top of the US singles chart.

### Girl power

Alanis Morissette was no newcomer to fame in the 1990s. As a child she had featured on the TV cable show *You Can't Do That On Television* and further acting roles as she grew up helped her finance her early recording career. By the 1990s, though, she had grown into an uncompromising and tough singer/songwriter. Morissette's 1995 album, *Jagged Little Pill*, was a million miles away from fellow starlet Britney Spear's bubblegum pop image, and won the Canadian two Grammy awards. The decade also saw the emegence of Sheryl Crow, an outspoken singer/songwriter very much in the mould of Morissette. One retail outlet even stopped selling Crow's records when she had the gall to criticise their policies, but her albums flew off the shelves elsewhere. By 1997 her sales had reached triple-platinum status.

The decade also a proved a rewarding one for Bonnie Rait. Her album *Nick Of Time* hit Number One on the US album chart in spring 1990 and was followed in 1991 with the Grammy-winning *Luck Of The Draw*. Raitt's recording career dated back to the 1970s, and in many ways she could consider herself to be the musical godmother of both Alanis Morissette and Sheryl Crow.

Other female artists chose to tread safer territories. Celine Dion's *Titanic* love theme 'My Heart Will Go On', was a classic pop epic, melting the iciest heart. The song helped make the *Titanic* sountrack and Dion's own album *Let's Talk About Love,* into multi-platinum best sellers.

**Boy bands**

The 1990s also had its fair share of boy bands. The decade's pre-eminant example, the Backstreet Boys, were named after Backstreet

Female solo artists dominated the 1990s album market, but the Dixie Chicks' Grammy-winning album, *Wide Open Spaces*, showed that girl bands could top the charts too.

Market, a shopping area in Orlando, Florida. Legend has it that Backstreet Boys landed a major recording deal after their co-manager, Donna Wright, phoned a Jive Records executive on her mobile from one of their early concerts. The executive heard the screaming crowd and the band was signed up the very next day.

The 1990s saw a plethora of former television child stars grow up and turn into hot chart material. Two members of *N Sync, the decade's other chart-topping boy band, had cut their teeth working on the Disney Channel's *Mickey Mouse Club*, as had Britney Spears. Spears and *N Sync's Justin Timberlake later starting dating, and the antics of the two young pop icons were destined to fuel the gossip columns for years.

### Brit-pop

In the UK, the Spice Girls were formed as the answer to British boy bands such as Take That and belted out a fistful of punchy songs, attracting worldwide interest. But anyone who expected a return to the days when British music dominated the charts would be disappointed. On an international scale the Brit-pop boom of the mid-90s created ripples rather than tidal waves and many British artists found it difficult to reach out across the Atlantic. One of the great exceptions to this was Oasis. In 1994 the group won the best UK band category in the MTV European music awards and in 1996 their album *(What's The Story) Morning Glory?* slid into the US album chart at Number Four. Unashamedly influenced by Lennon and McCartney, Oasis were hailed by some as the new Beatles, although many found their style too derivative.

Another British band to achieve significant US success were UK grunge-rockers Bush, although intriguingly the band were never accepted to quite the same extent in their homeland. Meanwhile Irish rock superstars U2 continued to receive critical acclaim, exploring dark themes with their ambitious 1991 album *Achtung Baby*, and Irish quartet The Cranberries charted strongly with 1994's *No Need To Argue*.

### Rockers and grungers

America had never really taken to punk, but kids in the 1990s were more than willing to embrace punk's more accessible offspring, grunge. The grunge-rock movement grew as a reaction to the surplus of complacent, well-groomed talent in the album chart. Suddenly, it was cool to upset your parents again.

The prime exponents of this music, such as godfathers of grunge Pearl Jam and Nirvana, came from Seattle. Pearl Jam's album, *Ten*, was close to selling 10,000,000 copies by August

1992 and Nirvana could boast similar sales with *Nevermind*. Tracks such as 'Smells Like Teen Spirit' and 'Come As You Are' from *Nevermind* became grunge anthems, with sales later fuelled undoubtedly by Kurt Cobain's suicide in April 1994, when he blasted himself with a shotgun.

Meanwhile the 1980s stadium-rock bands such as Bon Jovi and Def Leppard were increasingly sidelined by the new heavy metal movement represented by bands like Metallica. Some of Metallica's shows were more like battlefields than concerts. In a March 1992 concert in Florida, Metallica fans dangled a security guard by his ankles from the balcony. Four months later, Metallica guitarist and vocalist James Hetfield was rushed to hospital suffering from serious burns after a stage effect exploded during a concert in Montreal. Hetfield recovered, although accidents and controversy continued to follow the band. Nonetheless, Metallica's album sales remained huge. In 1999, the RIAA gave them a diamond award for selling more than 10,000,000 copies of their album, *Metallica*.

Nirvana's 1991 album *Nevermind* turned frontman Kurt Cobain into a major rock icon and paved the way for the explosion of grunge bands in the mid-1990s.

## Rap and R&B

The 1990s saw fresh developments in rap music, hip hop and R&B which would feed the record industry for many years to come. The first moves were made by Vanilla Ice and MC Hammer, whose album, *Please Hammer Don't Hurt 'Em,* was recorded for a lowly $10,000 but spent 21 weeks at the top of the album chart. Advertisers were quick to pick up on the marketing potential offered by dance music. MC Hammer signed a deal with British Knights athletic footwear and Pepsi-Cola. Several other artists also signed lucrative sponsorship deals.

The huge success of albums such as *Music Box* made Mariah Carey the decade's pre-eminent R&B star.

## Bad boys

Although hip-hop and R&B became increasingly bankable, the music had more than its fair share of trouble in the 1990s. Among other incidents, Whitney Houston's husband Bobby Brown faced drug and assault charges, Boyz II Men's tour manager was gunned down and killed in Chicago and R. Kelly had to cancel a big concert when he and his entourage were involved in a brawl.

The gangsta-rap movement of the late 1980s played out to its logical conclusion in 1996–97 with the violent deaths of two of hip hop's biggest stars, Tupac Shakur and the Notorious B.I.G. Their deaths did little to dent the music's popularity. The Notorious B.I.G's murder boosted sales of his posthumously released album *Life After Death* over the 10,000,000 mark and inspired Puff Daddy's tribute 'I'll be missing You'.

But 1990s hip hop and R&B had much more to offer than gangstas and drive-by shootings. The Fugees debut album *The Score*, provided a welcome antidote to the macho-posturing of other 1990s rappers and their version of Roberta Flack's 1973 hit 'Killing Me Softly', became a classic lovers' anthem. *The Score* was named R&B album of the year at the 1996 Billboard Music Awards. Will Smith, meanwhile, proved that hip-hop didn't have to rely on violence or profanity to appeal to record buyers.

Mariah Carey, with her impish looks and a seven octave voice, became the best-selling R&B diva of the 1990s. Her three biggest albums of the decade sold more than 30,000,000 copies between them. Meanwhile R&B boy band Boyz II Men formed at Philadelphia's High School of Creative and Performing Arts, where their tight harmony style quickly gained them plenty of attention. Like Whitney Houston, Boyz II Men contributed to a couple of big movie hits – 'End Of The Road' was featured in the Eddie Murphy movie *Boomerang* and 'I Will Get There' was used on the soundtrack to *Prince Of Egypt*.

**Innovation and diversity**

The 1990s began with some commentators wondering whether the growing popularity of computer games would stop kids from spending money on music; the decade ended with many in the industry expressing concerns about the affects of illegal downloading on record sales. But 1990s music was anything but in a crisis – the album charts show an industry in fine health, in terms of both the profits and the quality and diversity of music available. The great virtue of 1990s music was that it never settled into a niche or grew complacent, but continued to innovate, constantly bringing new and different styles and sounds into the mainstream.

*The Miseducation Of Lauryn Hill*, a fluid blend of hip hop, soul and R&B, won Hill five Grammy awards (and six more nominations) to add to the two Grammy awards she had picked up with the Fugees for their 1996 album *The Score*.

# 100 Pure Country

| • **Album sales:** 6,000,000 | • **Release date:** September 1992 |

The early 1990s were something of a watershed for country music, the massive success of Garth Brooks signalling the emergence of a new generation of country stars. George Strait's more traditional brand of Texan swing – straight, no-frills country music – had little of Brook's hype or arena-rock tendencies. Yet he was one of the few country stars of the 1980s to continue to sell just as strongly throughout the next decade.

The album *Pure Country* was a soundtrack to a film of the same name, starring Strait as a disillusioned country superstar who retreats back to his roots in the heartlands of America. The film won Strait the Tex Ritter Award at the Academy of Country Music (ACM) awards. The music itself is an enticing mix of sentimental, fiddle-laden ballads such as 'When Did You Stop Loving Me' and uptempo, hard country tracks such as 'Thoughts Of A Fool' or 'Heartland'. The album reached the top of the country charts and peaked at Number Six on the pop charts. The Eric Kaz-composed single 'I Cross My Heart' topped the country singles charts for two weeks.

In 2003 Strait won an ACM Special Achievement Award in recognition of achieving 50 Number Ones. Such consistency only goes to show that, although fashions change, there is always room in the charts for some pure country.

**Number One singles:**
None

**Grammy awards:** None

**Label:** US: MCA UK: Universal IMS

**Recorded in:** N/A

**Producer:**
Tony Brown
Steve Dorff

**Personnel:**
George Strait
Andrea Zonn
Brent Mason
Brent Rowan
Buddy Eammons
Darren Smith
David Hungate
Dean Parks
Doug Livingston
Eddie Bayers
George Doering
Glen Duncan

1  Heartland  (2:16)
2  Baby Your Baby  (2:42)
3  I Cross My Heart  (3:30)
4  When Did You Stop Loving Me  (2:48)
5  She Lays It All On The Line  (2:30)
6  Overnight Male  (2:36)
7  Last In Love  (3:35)
8  Thoughts Of A Fool  (2:12)
9  King Of Broken Hearts  (3:08)
10  Where The Sidewalk Ends  (3:08)
11  Heartland (Main Title Sequence)  (2:42)

Total album length: 44 minutes

# GEORGE STRAIT

**PURE COUNTRY**

MCAD-10651

DDD

## ORIGINAL MOTION PICTURE SOUNDTRACK

# 99 Yes I Am

| • **Album sales:** 6,000,000 | • **Release date:** September 1993 |

Her fourth release, *Yes I Am* was Melissa Etheridge's breakthrough album and commercially her most successful. The title was widely taken to signal the singer publicly acknowledging her homosexuality for the first time. The sound was a powerful collection of anthemic blues rock, distinguished by her deep, rasping vocals and heartfelt lyrics.

Etheridge plays with the same group of musicians throughout – including prolific session guitarman Waddy Wachtel and ex-Small Face Ian McLagan – helping to give the album a concise, consistent tone. Producer Hugh Padgham, who

had worked extensively with Phil Collins and Sting, brought the same dynamic, commercial sense to this album. The opening track, 'I'm the Only One', is a defiant, churning rocker and sets the tone. 'If I Wanted,' 'All American Girl' and 'Resist' rock out in a similar style. Etheridge shows her subtler, more emotional side in tracks like the acoustic-based 'Come to My Window' and 'I Will Never Be The Same'.

*Yes I Am* reached Number 15 in the Billboard Top 200 and produced two Top 30 singles – 'I'm the Only One' and 'Come to My Window'. Both were nominated for Best Rock Song at the 1995 Grammy awards, at which Etheridge won the award for Best Female Vocal Rock Performance.

**Number One singles:**
None

**Grammy awards:** Best female rock vocal performance – Come To My Window

**Label:** US: Polygram; UK: Island

**Recorded in:**
Los Angeles, USA

**Personnel:**
Melissa Etheridge
Waddy Wachtel
James Fearnley
Ian McLagen
Scott Thurston
Pino Palladino
Kevin McCormick
David Sutton
Mauricio Fritz Lewak

**Producer:**
Hugh Padgham

1 I'm The Only One (4:54)
2 If I Wanted To (3:55)
3 Come to My Window (3:55)
4 Silent Legacy (5:22)
5 I Will Never Be The Same (4:41)
6 All American Girl (4:05)
7 Yes I Am (4:24)
8 Resist (2:57)
9 Ruins (4:53)
10 Talking To My Angel (4:48)

Total album length: 44 minutes

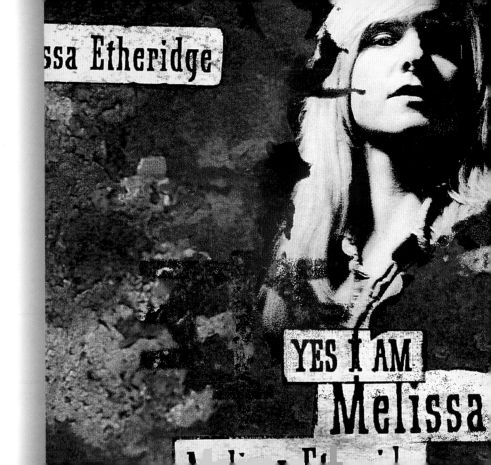

# 98 Donde Jugaran Los Ninos?

| • **Album sales:** 6,000,000 | • **Release date:** April 1994 |

Despite their Mexican roots, Mana owe a greater debt to straightforward pop-rock than the Latin rhythms of artists such as Ricky Martin. The band's unique sound and slick production values helped them to develop a passionate Latin American following several years before mainstream success beckoned. This popularity, and Mexico's thriving tourist industry, helped Mana achieve crossover success.

*Donde Jugaran Los Ninos?*, the band's second album, offered both catchy tunes and lyrics with a political message. While singer

Fher's western-styled vocals – drawing frequent comparison to Sting – provide one of Mana's main hooks, vocal duties are shared here, as on other albums, with drummer Alex. The title track translates as 'Where Will The Children Play?' and reflects the social conscience that underscores their music as strongly as their sense of rhythm. The track serves as a plea not to ruin the earth for future generations.

The album's success was in part fuelled by the band's vivid concerts, which had resulted in a surge in popularity as the 1980s drew to a close. *Donde Jugaran Los Ninos?* spent 97 consecutive weeks in Billboard's Latin Top 50, peaking at Number Four, and is regarded by many as the group's defining album.

**Number One singles:**
None

**Grammy awards:** None.

**Label:** US & UK: WEA

**Recorded in:**
Los Angeles, USA

**Personnel:**
Fher
Vampiro
Iván González
Juan Calleros
Alex González
Ramon Flores
Jose Quintana
Luis Conte
Sheila Rios

**Producers:**
Fher
Alex González
Jose Quintana

1  De Pies a Cabeza  (4:35)
2  Oye Mi Amor  (4:32)
3  Cachito  (4:46)
4  Vivir Sin Aire  (4:51)
5  Donde Jugaran los Ninos?  (4:14)
6  El Desierto  (4:09)
7  La Chula  (4:07)
8  Como Te Deseo  (4:30)
9  Te Lloré Un Rio  (4:52)
10  Como Diablos  (3:53)
11  Huele A Tristeza  (4:43)
12  Me Vale  (4:32)
13  Como Te Deseo [Remix Version]  (4:43)
14  La Chula [Remix Version]  (5:53)

Total album length: 64 minutes

# 97 Smash

| • Album sales: 6,000,000 | • Release date: April 1994 |

Afine example of the bold fusion of varied musical forms that would ultimately define 1990s pop, the release of Smash also cemented Offspring's status as a key rock group. The first single from the album, entitled 'Come Out And Play', first started to receive valuable airplay from the Los Angeles-based station KROQ, who were on the lookout for a suitably hard-edged band. Other radio stations soon joined in, and as MTV began to screen the promo, the group found themselves entering a new realm of popularity.

The album was completed in February 1994, with Thom Wilson (who had worked on both previous albums) once again producing. Overall, Smash marked a point of transition for Offspring with an audible shift from the raw punk of their earlier recordings to a cleaner, more radio-friendly sound that still succeeded in breaking a few musical boundaries.

Perhaps not suspecting the attention Smash would receive, Offspring wrote only 12 songs for the album – all of which appear on the final recording. However one member of the band, at least, was confident that Smash would be a hit: bassist Greg Kriesel resigned from his printing job the day before the album was released. Sure enough, Smash went on to set a new record for sales of an independent album and stayed on the charts for nearly two years, peaking at Number Four on the Billboard Top 200.

| | |
|---|---|
| **Number One singles:** None | **Personnel:** Dexter Holland Noodles |
| **Grammy awards:** None | Greg K Ron Welty |
| **Label:** US & UK: Epitaph | Jason McLean |
| **Recorded in:** North Hollywood, USA | **Producer:** Thom Wilson |

1 Time to Relax (0:25)
2 Nitro (Youth Energy) (2:25)
3 Bad Habit (3:43)
4 Gotta Get Away (3:52)
5 Genocide (3:33)
6 Something To Believe In (3:17)
7 Come Out And Play (3:17)
8 Self-Esteem (4:17)

9 It'll Be A Long Time (2:43)
10 Killboy Powerhead (2:02)
11 What Happened to You? (2:12)
12 So Alone (1:17)
13 Not The One (2:54)
14 Smash (10:42)

Total album length: 47 minutes

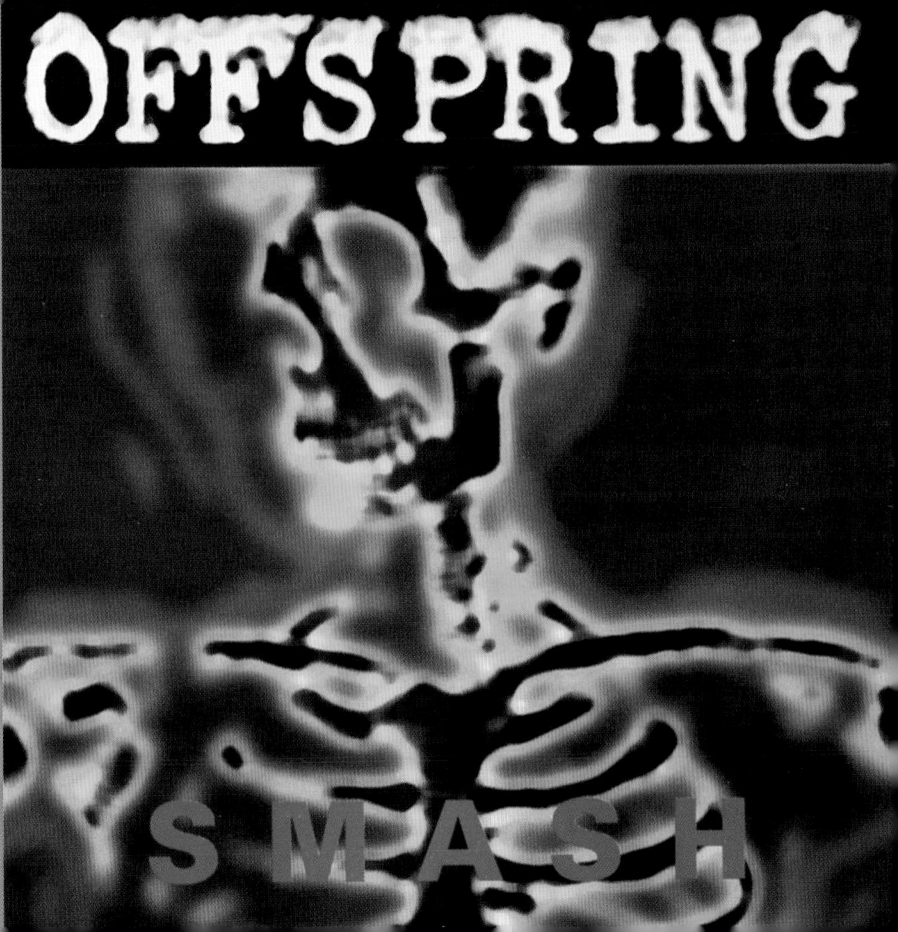
OFFSPRING
SMASH

**• Album sales:** 6,000,000 **• Release date:** September 1994

The band's fourth album, the appropriately titled *Four*, was a major breakthrough album for Blues Traveler. Although the blues band had developed its skills and reputation through years of touring, with their harmonica-infused blues-rock gaining fans wherever they travelled, it wasn't until their 1995 single 'Run Around' was released that they launched into mainstream recognition. The song became one of the biggest singles of 1995 (with nearly a year in the charts, the single is now unofficially the longest serving record on the US charts).

The sleeve image for the album came about after an incident early in Blues Traveler's career. Following a recorded rehearsal in New Jersey, the band was joined by a black cat while listening to the tape. Once the music ended the cat departed, inspiring the band to adopt the attentive feline's image as their long-running mascot, and eventually hiring an artist friend to design the album cover.

The album's closing track, 'Brother John', was written by the late bassist Bobby Sheehan about his own younger brother, whose personal problems foreshadowed Bobby's own drug overdose in August 1999.

Two years after its release, *Four* was still on the US charts, having amassed over 4,000,000 sales. The album managed to reach Number Eight in the US, but failed to chart in the UK.

**Number One singles:**
None

**Grammy awards:** Best Rock Performance by a Duo or Group With Vocal

**Label:** US: A&M; UK: Polydor

**Recorded in:**
Woodstock, USA

**Personnel:**
John Popper
Chan Kinchla
Bobby Sheehan (d. 1999)
Brendan Hill
Jono Manson
Warren Haynes
Peter Malcolm Kavakavich
Chuck Leavell
Paul Shaffer
Bashiri Johnson

**Producer:**
Steve Thompson
Michael Barbiero

1  Run-Around (4:40)
2  Stand (5:19)
3  Look Around (5:42)
4  Fallible (4:47)
5  The Mountains Win Again (5:06)
6  Freedom (4:01)
7  Crash Burn (2:59)
8  Price To Pay (5:17)
9  Hook (4:49)
10 The Good, The Bad, And The Ugly (1:55)
11 Just Wait (5:34)
12 Brother John (6:38)

Total album length: 57 minutes

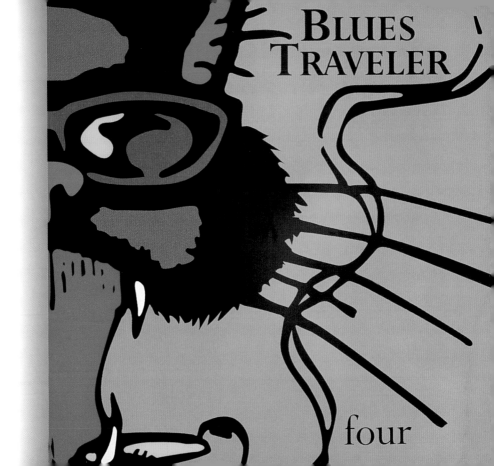

# 95 Under The Table And Dreaming

| • **Album sales:** 6,000 000 | • **Release date:** September 1994 |

Hailing from a Virginia and, some would argue, filling the void left in the wake of groups like the Grateful Dead and the Allman Brothers Band, Dave Matthews Band rose quickly to attention following their formation in 1990.

A heady and eclectic mix of jazz, world music, folk, and rock sounds drawn from an unconventional range of instruments, together with a busy touring schedule, saw the major labels bidding against one another to sign the band up. Eventually RCA won the deal, offering greater flexibility than the other labels. The formalities out of the way, Dave Matthews Band followed their self-released live debut with *Under The Table And Dreaming*. Matthews dedicated the album to his sister, who had been murdered in his native South Africa.

The second track, 'What Would You Say?', became the band's first hit single, gaining airplay across rock and pop radio, as well as on MTV. Other singles, 'Ants Marching' and 'Satellite', would become huge live favourites.

Another busy touring schedule helped the album achieve Number Two on the Billboard Top 200, and over 1,000,000 sales in less than a year. Before the follow-up album, *Crash*, was released, *Under The Table And Dreaming* was certified three times platinum.

**Number One singles:**
None

**Grammy awards:** None

**Label:** US & UK: RCA

**Recorded in:**
Bearsville, USA

**Producer:**
Steve Lillywhite

**Personnel:**
David Matthews
Boyd Tinsley
Leroi Moore
Carter Beauford
Stefan Lessard
John Alagia
Andrew Page
Jeff Thomas
Michael McDonald
Tim Reynolds
John Popper
Steve Forman

1 The Best Of What's Around (4:17)
2 What Would You Say (3:42)
3 Satellite (4:51)
4 Rhyme & Reason (5:15)
5 Typical Situation (5:59)
6 Dancing Nancies (6:05)
7 Ants Marching (4:31)
8 Lover Lay Down (5:37)
9 Jimi Thing (5:57
10 Warehouse (7:06)
11 Pay For What You Get (4:32)
12 #34 (5:00)

Total album length: 63 minutes

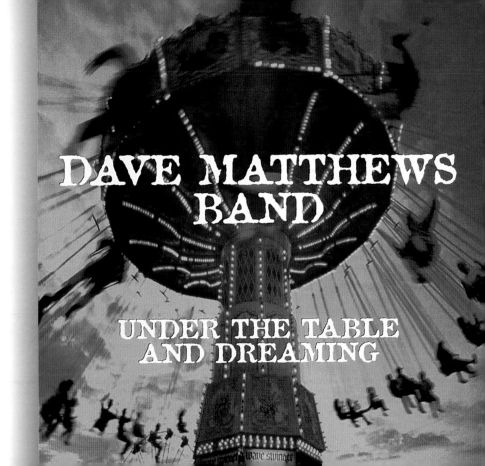

# 94 Sixteen Stone

| • Album sales: 6,000,000 | • Release date: December 1994 |

A rare case of a British band whose US success eclipsed their domestic impact, Bush managed to sign an American record label deal without even having a UK deal in place. Strong US sales of *Sixteen Stone* eventually helped Bush acquire a British contract, if not comparable success.

Predominantly written by frontman Gavin Rossdale, *Sixteen Stone* explores universal issues such as sex, death and religion, as well as home-grown concerns like the bombing of a Covent Garden pub in 'Bomb'. However, it was the group's cleaned-up, Nirvana-inspired, grunge sound that the US audience really tuned into.

Ironically for such a US-styled band, production duties on their debut album were performed by the partnership of Clive Langer and Alan Winstanley. The pair had made their name producing such British musical icons as Madness, Elvis Costello and Lloyd Cole and the Commotions. *Sixteen Stone* was released to generally negative reviews, but the video for the single 'Everything Zen' became an MTV favourite and helped the album achieve gold status.

The second single, 'Little Things', made Number Four in the Billboard Modern Rock Chart, whilst subsequent singles, 'Comedown' and 'Glycerine', both reached Number One.

**Number One singles:**
None

**Grammy awards:** None

**Label:** US: Trauma; UK: Atlantic

**Recorded in:**
Woodstock, USA

**Personnel:**
Gavin Rossdale
Nigel Pulsford
Dave Parsons
Robin Goodridge

Jasmine Lewis
Alessandro Vittorio Tateo Winston
Gavin Wright
Carolina Dale
Vincas Bundza

**Producers:**
Clive Langer
Alan Winstanley
Gavin Rossdale
Nigel Pulsford
Dave Parsons
Robin Goodridge

1 Everything Zen (4:38)
2 Swim (4:55)
3 Bomb (3:22)
4 Little Things (4:24)
5 Comedown (5:26)
6 Body (5:42)
7 Machinehead (4:16)
8 Testosterone (4:19)
9 Monkey (4:00)
10 Glycerine (4:26)
11 Alien (6:34)
12 X-Girlfriend (0:45)

Total album length: 53 minutes

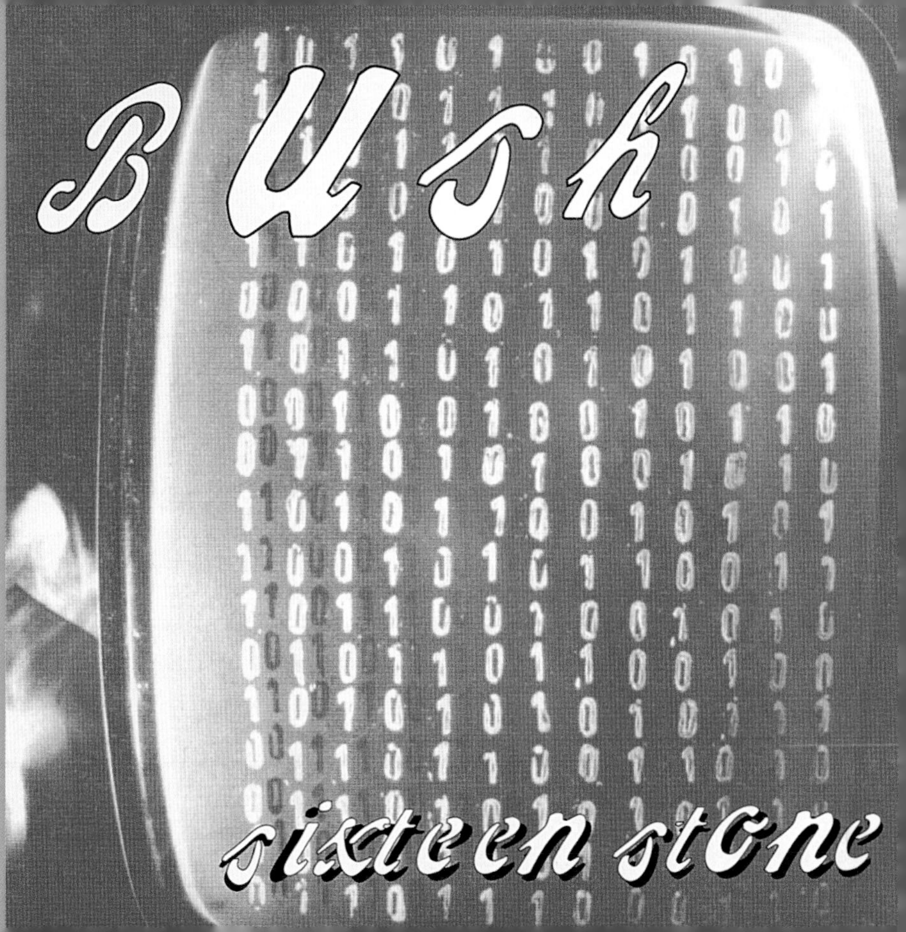
Bush
sixteen stone

# 93 Blue

| • Album sales: 6,000,000 | • Release date: July 1996 |

A combination of canny PR and natural talent made LeAnn Rimes an instant country star while just a teenager. Promoter Bill Mack had discovered Rimes when she was only 11 and earmarked a song he had written during the 1960s, 'Blue', as the perfect showcase for her talents. Mack's story was that he had written 'Blue' for Patsy Cline, but the country legend had died before recording it. Since then he had been waiting for Cline's successor to come along. While the press absorbed the story wholesale, the truth was that the song had been recorded by three different artists since the 1960s. Still, 'Blue' proved the perfect choice to launch Rimes' career and establish her as a major country star.

The song broke a new record for a country music single by selling more than 100,000 copies during its first week on release. It also earned Rimes two Grammys and a nomination for Country Music Association Best Country Singer – making Rimes the youngest artist ever to receive a CMA nomination. *Blue* reached Number Three on the Billboard Top 200.

**Number One singles:**
None

**Grammy awards:**
Best new artist; Best female country vocal performance – Blue

**Label:** US & UK: Curb

**Recorded in:** Clovis & Nashville, USA

**Personnel:**
LeAnn Rimes
Eddy Arnold
Johnny Mulhair
Jerry Matheny
M. Spriggs
Dan Huff
Brent Rowan
John Jorgenson
Milo Deering
Bruce Bouton
Paul Franklin
Larry Franklin
Kevin Bailey
Paul Goad
Jimmy Kelly
Mike McLain
John Hobbs
Steve Nathan
Kelly Glenn
Curtis Randel
Mike Chapman
Glenn Worf
Bob Smith
Fred Gleber
Brad Billingsley
Greg Morrow
Chad Cromwell
Terry McMillan
Joy McKay
Perry Coleman
Mary Ann Kennedy
Various other personnel

**Producer:**
Wilbur C. Rimes
Chuck Howard

1  Blue (2:47)
2  Hurt Me (2:53)
3  One Way Ticket (Because I Can) (3:52)
4  My Baby (2:49)
5  Honestly (3:21)
6  The Light In Your Eyes (3:20)
7  Talk To Me (3:11)
8  I'll Get Even With You (3:18)
9  Cattle Call (3:07)
10 Good Lookin' Man (3:11)
11 Fade To Blue (3:03)

Total album length: 34 minutes

LeAnn Rimes

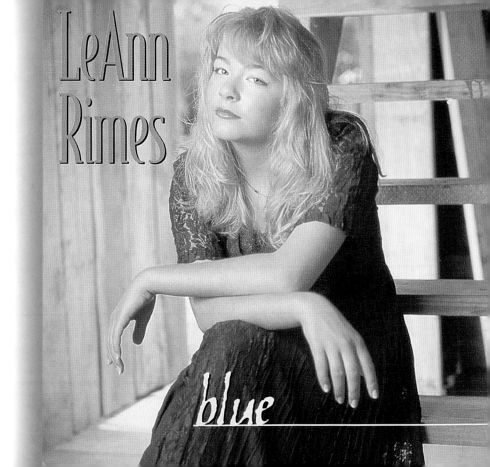

# 92 Third Eye Blind

| • **Album sales:** 6,000,000 | • **Release date:** April 1997 |

A bidding war erupted around the as yet unsigned Third Eye Blind prior to the release of their debut album. This was fuelled mainly by frontman Stephan Jenkins' producing skills (as evidenced on The Braids' cover version of 'Bohemian Rhapsody') and an impressive 1996 live performance opening for Oasis.

The group ultimately went with Elektra, whose CEO, Sylvia Rhodes, had actively demonstrated her support. The label proved willing to not only allow Jenkins to produce the debut album, but also signed him to help nurture other new bands.

Jenkins credits the four years it took to gain a contract as a contributing factor to the strength of their debut album. Of the 14 songs that were recorded, many originated from a 14-track demo that the group had used to gain attention. Engineer Eric Valentine, who had also helped produce the group's demos, was retained for the album. The final line-up was rehearsed in a San Francisco warehouse before being taken into the studio.

Ironically, the band's name and reputation were made with the single that least represented the album, 'Semi-Charmed Life', which became an MTV favourite despite the subject matter concerning addiction to speed. *Third Eye Blind* reached Number 25 on the Billboard Top 200.

**Number One singles:**
None

**Grammy awards:** None

**Label:** US & UK: Elektra

**Recorded in:**
California, USA

**Personnel:**
Stephan Jenkins
Kevin Cadogan
Arion Salazar
Brad Hargreaves
Eric Valentine
Ari Gorman
Michael Urbano

**Producers:**
Ren Klyce
Eric Valentine
Stephan Jenkins
Kevin Cadogan

1 **Losing A Whole Year** (3:20)
2 **Narcolepsy** (3:48)
3 **Semi-Charmed Life** (4:28)
4 **Jumper** (4:32)
5 **Graduate** (3:09)
6 **How's It Going To Be** (4:13)
7 **Thanks A Lot** (4:57)
8 **Burning Man** (2:59)
9 **Good For You** (3:52)
10 **London** (3:07)
11 **I Want You** (4:29)
12 **The Background** (4:56)
13 **Motorcycle Drive By** (4:22)
14 **God Of Wine** (5:17)

Total album length: 57 minutes

**Third Eye Blind**

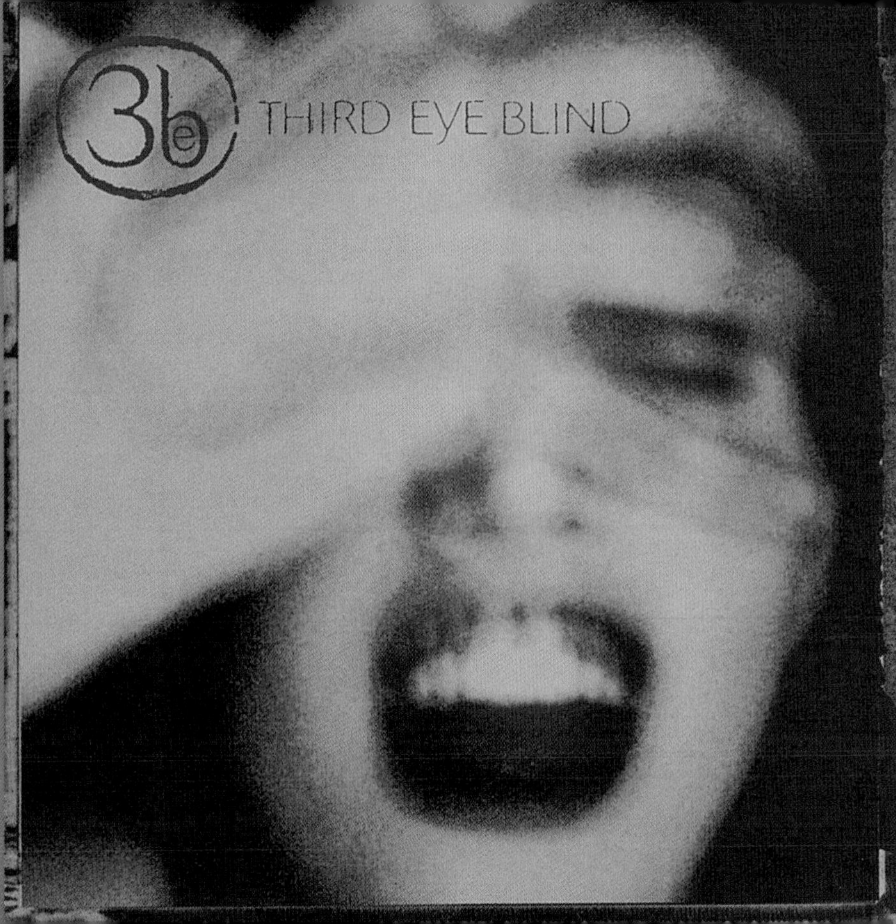
THIRD EYE BLIND

# 91 My Own Prison

| • **Album sales:** 6,000,000 | • **Release date:** June 1997 |

Creed's debut album, *My Own Prison*, was originally recorded for less than $6000, but took under two years to reach triple-platinum status. Initially released independently, the album was remixed (by Soundgarden producer Ron Saint-Germain, who introduced a heavier, more radio-friendly sound) and re-released by Wind-Up records six months later.

Frontman Scott Stapp had been raised in a strictly religious household in which rock music was forbidden. After he left home he wrote most of the lyrics for *My Own Prison* in his car, which doubled as his temporary home. Ultimately, Stapp's religious background found its way into the songs, the subject matter of which tended towards both spiritual and social concerns, although never at the expense of Creed's straightforward, post-grunge rock sound.

Although the album peaked at Number 22 in the Billboard Top 200, sales of *My Own Prison* remained very strong with the release of four successful singles ('My Own Prison', 'Torn', 'What's This Life For, and 'One') pushing the album on to greater heights. Although the band received relatively little support from MTV or the mainstream media, this failed to impact on album sales, with more than 5,000,000 copies of *My Own Prison* selling before the decade was up.

**Number One singles:**
None

**Grammy awards:** None

**Label:** US: Wind-Up;
UK: Epic

**Recorded in:** Tallahassee
& Miami, USA

**Personnel:**
Mark Tremonti
Scott Stapp
Brian Marshall
Scott Phillips
John Kurzweg

**Producer:**
John Kurzweg

1 Torn (6:23)
2 Ode (4:57)
3 My Own Prison (4:58)
4 Pity For A Dime (5:29)
5 In America (4:58)
6 Illusion (4:37)
7 Unforgiven (3:38)
8 Sister (4:56)
9 What's This Life For (4:08)
10 One (5:02)

Total album length: 54 minutes

CREED

my own prison

# 90 12 Play

| • **Album sales:** 6,100,000 | • **Release date:** November 1993 |

R. Kelly's second album, *12 Play*, marked a turning point for the controversial R&B artist. Kelly not only performed vocal duties, but also produced, mixed, arranged and played many of the instruments. While some of the tracks indicate a sentimental side, such as 'Sadie', which concerned Kelly's late mother, he makes more frequent overtures to the habitual themes of sex and violence. The more salacious subject matter helped several singles from *12 Play* to place in the charts during 1993 and 1994. 'Sex Me, Pts. 1-2' went gold, while the following year saw Kelly reach Number One on four separate Billboard charts with 'Bump n'Grind', including a 12-week run at the top of the R&B chart. The third single, 'Your Body's Callin' peaked at Number 13 on the US singles chart.

More importantly, *12 Play* helped R. Kelly emerge from his new jack-swing roots, achieve crossover success and become one of the biggest selling male acts of the decade. The album reached Number Two on the Billboard chart, peaking at Number 39 in the UK. The album also re-entered the UK chart at Number 20 two years later in 1995.

**Number One singles:**
US: Bump n' Grind

**Grammy awards:** None

**Label:** US & UK: Jive

**Recorded at:**
Chicago, USA

**Producers:**
Ray Kelley
R. Kelly
Timmy Allen

**Personnel:**
R. Kelly
DeAndre Boykins
Carey Kelly
Bobby Broom
Michael J Powell
Mike Logan
Jim Slattery
Timmy Allen
Ron Hall
Yvonne Gage
Robin Robinson

1 **Your Body's Callin'** (4:37)
2 **Bump n' Grind** (4:15)
3 **Homie Lover Friend** (4:22)
4 **It Seems Like You're Ready** (4:38)
5 **Freak Dat Body** (3:43)
6 **I Like the Crotch on You** (6:37)
7 **Summer Bunnies** (4:14)
8 **For You** (5:01)
9 **Back to the Hood of Things** (3:52)
10 **Sadie** (4:30)
11 **Sex Me, Pts. 1-2** (11:27)
12 **12 Play** (5:57)

Total album length: 63 minutes

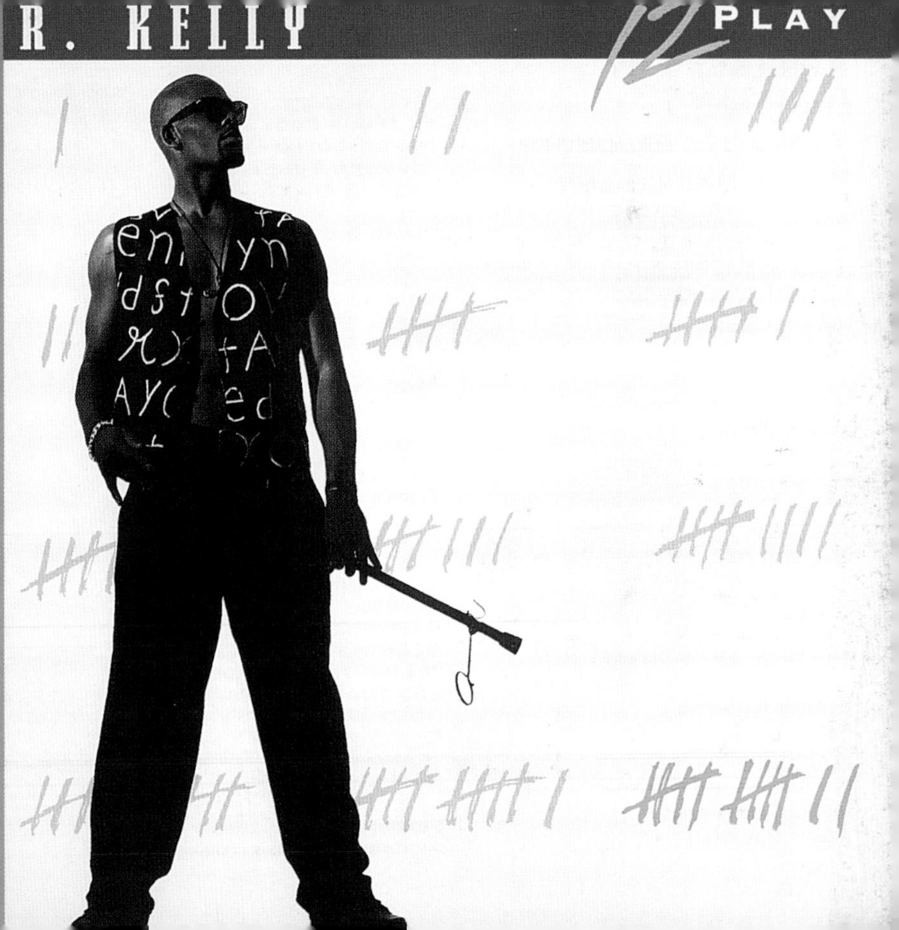
R. KELLY
12 PLAY

# 89 Purple

| • Album sales: 6,100,000 | • Release date: May 1994 |

After enduring criticism for their debut album, *Core*, which many felt owed a few too many debts to other grunge pioneers, Stone Temple Pilots made a conscious effort to distinguish themselves with *Purple*. The vilification continued, but *Purple* still debuted at Number One in the Billboard chart, and remained there for three weeks. In the UK the album reached the Number Ten spot.

Under the guidance of producer Brendan O'Brien, Stone Temple Pilots managed to record and mix *Purple* in the space of three weeks. They had spent a year and a half touring *Core*, and had used the sound checks to work on new material. By the time the group hit the studio again, they had somewhere in the region of forty new songs to pick from. Partially escaping their grunge background, the group forged ahead with a harder rock sound, mixing strong riffs while never shying from occasional acoustic moments. Cuts such as 'Big Empty' and 'Interstate Love Song' are considered to be amongst the band's finest work. *Purple* also includes a hidden twelfth track, '12 Gracious Melodies'.

The commercial success of *Purple,* and the freedom it granted for the group to take a break, would take its toll with singer Scott Weiland developing a heroin addiction in the years following the album's release.

| Number One singles: | Personnel: |
|---|---|
| None | Scott Weiland |
| | Dean DeLeo |
| **Grammy awards:** None | Robert DeLeo |
| | Eric Kretz |
| **Label**: US & UK: Atlantic | Paul Leary |
| | Brendan O'Brien |
| **Recorded in:** | |
| Minneapolis, USA | **Producer:** |
| | Brendan O'Brien |

1　Meat Plow  (3:37)
2　Vasoline  (2:56)
3　Lounge Fly  (5:18)
4　Interstate Love Song  (3:14)
5　Still Remains  (3:33)
6　Pretty Penny  (3:42)
7　Silver Gun Superman  (5:16)
8　Big Empty  (4:54)
9　Unglued  (2:34)
10　Army Ants  (3:46)
11　Kitchen Ware & Candy Bars  (8:06)

Total album length: 47 minutes

# 88 Fresh Horses

| • **Album sales:** 6,100,000 | • **Release date:** November 1995 |

By 1995 it seemed clear that while Garth Brooks was one of the biggest acts in the US, he would never reclaim the heights of his earlier albums. The previous two years had been bereft of new material in the US, with only a limited edition greatest hits album to remind the public why they had fallen for him in the first place. Meanwhile, the country singer had, against the odds, managed to make his mark in the UK. *Fresh Horses*, therefore, was Brooks' first album to warrant a simultaneous worldwide release. It also marked one of his occasional attempts to extend the boundaries of his country music pigeon-hole, most notably with a cover version of Aerosmith's 'The Fever'.

Reportedly, Brooks found *Fresh Horses* to be one of his hardest albums to record, due in part to a lengthy absence from the studio. A further factor was the personal nature of several songs, eight of which were co-written by the singer. 'She's Every Woman' pays stylistic tribute to James Taylor, a musical hero, and became the first single. Meanwhile, the Oklahoma bombing, an event which occurred within a few miles of Brooks' parents, is tackled in 'The Change'.

Despite several million sales, *Fresh Horses* was considered something of a disappointment. The album reached Number Two on the Billboard Top 200 and peaked at Number 22 in the UK.

**Number One singles:**
None

**Grammy awards:** None

**Label:** US & UK: Capitol

**Recorded in:**
Nashville, USA

**Personnel:**
Garth Brooks
Mark Casstevens
Leigh Reynolds
Chris Leuzinger
Gordon Kennedy
Bruce Bouton
Rob Hajacos
Jimmy Mattingly
Ed Foote
Bobby Wood
Mike Chapman
Milton Sledge
Sam Bacco
Trisha Yearwood
Susan Ashton
Various other personnel

**Producer:**
Allen Reynolds

1 The Old Stuff (4:12)
2 Cowboys And Angels (3:16)
3 The Fever (2:40)
4 That Ol' Wind (5:22)
5 Rollin' (4:07)
6 The Change (4:06)
7 The Beaches of Cheyenne (4:13)
8 To Make You Feel My Love (3:55)
9 It's Midnight Cinderella (2:23)
10 She's Every Woman (5:01)
11 Ireland (2:53)

Total album length: 42 minutes

# 87 Space Jam

| • **Album sales:** 6,100,000 | • **Release date:** November 1996 |

The soundtrack to *Space Jam* – the live action/animation film featuring basketball star Michael Jordan and a host of Looney Tunes characters – represents the modern trend for broadening a film's appeal through careful marketing of the album. Indeed, a number of tracks featured in the film don't even make it onto the album, which instead favours a more marketable mix of gentle R&B, light hip hop and straightforward pop.

The album was just one part of huge media-wide *Space Jam* event. Warner tied in the launch of a new toy division and the opening of the New York Warner Brothers store to the release of the movie and album. Powered by R Kelly's smash hit 'I Believe I Can Fly', the *Space Jam* soundtrack reached Number Two in the US and peaked at Number Five in the UK.

**Number One singles:**
None

**Grammy awards:** Best male R&B performance; Best R&B song; Best song written for a motion picture or for television – I Believe I Can Fly

**Label:** US & UK: Atlantic

**Recorded in:**
Various locations

**Personnel:**
Chris Rock
Seal
Barry White
David Foster
Coolio
R Kelly
Biz Markie

Busta Rhymes
LL Cool J
Method Man
D'Angelo
Monica
Robin S
Various other personnel

**Producers:**
Seal
Brian Dobbs
Jay McGowan
C C Lemonhead
David Foster
Rashad Smith
Armando Colon
Todd Terry
Lou Adler
Jamey Jaz
Jimmy Jam
Terry Lewis
R Kelly
Various other producers

1 **Fly Like An Eagle** (Seal) (4:14)
2 **Winner** (Coolio) (4:03)
3 **Space Jam** (Quad City DJ's) (5:07)
4 **I Believe I Can Fly** (R Kelly) (5:22)
5 **Hit 'Em High** (B Real) (4:17)
6 **I Found My Smile Again** (D'Angelo) (6:15)
7 **For You I Will** (Monica) (4:56)
8 **Upside Down** (Salt-N-Pepa) (4:16)
9 **Givin' U All That I've Got** (Robin S) (4:04)
10 **Basketball Jones** (Chris Rock) (5:40)
11 **I Turn To You** (All-4-One) (4:52)
12 **All Of My Days** (Changing Faces) (4:01)
13 **That's The Way (I Like It)** (Biz Markie) (3:49)
14 **Buggin'** (Billy West) (4:14)

Total album length: 65 minutes

SPACE JAM

MUSIC FROM AND INSPIRED BY THE MOTION PICTURE

# 86 My Way

| • Album sales: 6,100,000 | • Release date: September 1997 |

Usher had had little trouble seducing record buyers with his soulful vocals on his 1994 debut album, but disappointing sales and lack of creative control encouraged him to take the reigns with his second effort. Having graduated from high school, the youthful hip-hop artist was ready to embrace his career fulltime and co-wrote six of the album's nine tracks. He was also able to bring in top-level talents including Babyface, Teddy Riley and Jermaine Dupri as co-writers and producers. Dupri's commitment to representing Usher's voice on *My Way* even extended to him living with the artist for a time.

The mixture of ballads and funk-tinged R&B not only brought Usher back into the R&B fold with a bang, but also helped him achieve crossover success. The first single, 'You Make Me Wanna', made Number One in the UK and remained at the top spot in the *Billboard* Hot R&B chart in the US for 11 weeks. The single was certified double platinum, while subsequent singles, 'Nice & Slow' and 'My Way' also reached platinum status. Usher's album reached Number Four on the Billboard Top 200 and peaked at Number 16 in the UK.

**Number One singles:** UK: You Make Me Wanna

**Grammy awards:** None

**Label:** US & UK: LaFace

**Recorded in:** College Park, New York, Los Angeles & Virgina Beach, USA

**Personnel:**
Usher
Monica
Lil' Kim
Jermaine Dupri
Manuel Seal
Greg Phillinganes
Babyface
Nathan East
Randy Walker
Jagged Edge
Trey Lorenz
Trina Broussard
Shanice Wilson

**Producers:**
Babyface
Jermaine Dupri
Sprauge Williams
Manuel Seal Jr

1  You Make Me Wanna  (3:39)
2  Just Like Me  (3:26)
3  Nice And Slow  (3:48)
4  Slow Jam  (4:40)
5  My Way  (3:38)
6  Come Back  (3:47)
7  I Will  (3:55)
8  Bedtime  (4:45)
9  One Day You'll Be Mine  (3:24)
10 You Make Me Wanna [Extended Version]  (5:20)

Total album length: 40 minutes

Usher
*My Way*

# 85 2001

**• Album sales:** 6,100,000 **• Release date:** November 1999

One of the founding members of the gangsta rap movement in the 1980s, Dr. Dre all but disappeared during the 1990s, although his influence was still prevalent. He re-emerged in 1999 with a new discovery, Eminem, and a new album. Although time and controversy had done nothing to dilute his musical skills, the tone of *2001* is more personal and occasionally mellow. Dre's defensive tone throughout reveals that his critics' words have had their impact.

Nearly one hundred songs were recorded for potential inclusion on the album, but it was the second-to-last recording that became the first single. The affirmative 'Still D R E' featured Snoop Dogg, and was selected by Dre as the perfect song to represent the album.

*2001* peaked at Number Two on the *Billboard* Top 200 and reached Number Four in the UK.

**Number One singles:**
None

**Grammy awards:** Best rap performance by a duo or group – Forgot About Dre; Producer of the year

**Label:** US: Aftermath; UK: Interscope

**Recorded in:** N/A

**Personnel:**
Dr. Dre
Snoop Dogg
Eminem
Hittman
Kurupt
Nate Dogg
King T
Sticky Fingas
Ms Roq
RBX
DeFari
Xzibit
Knoc-Turn'al
Six-Two
Eddie Griffin
MC Ren
Kokane
Rell
Traci Nelson
Jake Steed
Time Bomb
Devin AKA The Dude
Mary J Blige
Tray-Dee
Aaron Harris
Laylow
Sean Cruise
Carl Breeding
Scott Stocrch
Camara Kambon
Various other personnel

**Producer:**
Dr. Dre
Chris Taylor
Mel-Man

1 Lolo (Intro) (0:41)
2 The Watcher (3:26)
3 Fuck You (3:26)
4 Still D R E (4:30)
5 Big Ego's (3:58)
6 Xxplosive (3:35)
7 What's The Difference (4:04)
8 Bar One (0:50)
9 Light Speed (2:40)
10 Forgot About Dre (3:42)
11 The Next Episode (2:41)
12 Let's Get High (2:27)
13 Bitch Niggaz (4:13)
14 The Car Bomb (1:00)
15 Murder Ink8 (2:28)
16 Ed-Ucation (1:32)
17 Some L.A. Niggaz (4:25)
18 Pause 4 Porno (1:32)
19 Housewife (4:02)
20 Ackrite (3:39)
21 Bang Bang (4:02)
22 The Message (5:29)

Total album length: 68 minutes

DR. DRE

PARENTAL
ADVISORY
EXPLICIT CONTENT

 2001

# 84 Fanmail

| • **Album sales:** 6,300,000 | • **Release date:** February 1999 |

Although a variety of ills, including contractual disputes, legal wrangles and bankruptcy, delayed the production of *Fanmail*, an impressive list of contributors and producers was brought in to make sure that it was worth the four-year wait since 1994's release *CrazySexyCool*.

While the album failed to break any new ground, it did ensure that TLC retained their status as America's leading female R&B act. The inclusion of fans' names on an inner sleeve collage broadcast the fact that this was an album for those who had supported the trio. True to form the trio still had plenty to say. The US hit 'Unpretty', condemned the obsession with physical beauty, while neglecting inner beauty.

The album went straight to the top of the Billboard album chart, a remarkable feat considering the group had yet to release the requisite MTV-friendly video to drive sales, and peaked at Number Seven in the UK.

**Number One singles:**
US: No Scrubs; Unpretty

**Grammy awards:** Best R&B performance by a duo or group with vocal – No Scrubs; best R&B album

**Label:** US: La Face; UK: Arista

**Recorded in:** N/A

**Personnel:**
Tionne 'T-Boz' Watkins
Lisa Lopes (d. 2002)
Rozonda 'Chilli' Thomas
Vic-E
Jimmy Jam
Terry Lewis
Babyface
Michael Thompson

Mike Scott
Tomi Martin
Greg Phillinganes
Jerry Lumpkins
Debra Killings
C C Thomas
Lamarquis Jefferson
Nathan East
Colin Wolfe
Tim Knight
Paulinho Da Costa
Alex Richbourg
Dallas Austin
Leslie Brathwaite
Ty-Hudson

**Producers:**
Cyptron
Dallas Austin
Babyface
Jimmy Jam
Terry Lewis

1 Fanmail (3:59)
2 The Vic-E Interpertation (Interlude) (0:18)
3 Silly Ho (4:15)
4 Whispering Playa (Interlude) (0:52)
5 No Scrubs (3:34)
6 I'm Good At Being Bad (5:52)
7 If They Knew (4:04)
8 I Miss You So Much (4:56)
9 Unpretty (4:38)
10 My Life (4:01)
11 Shout (3:57)
12 Come On Down (4:17)
13 Dear Lie (5:10)
14 Communicate (Interlude) (0:51)
15 Lovesick (3:52)
16 Automatic (4:31)
17 Don't Pull Out On Me Yet (4:33)

Total album length: 64 minutes

TLC

FANMAIL

# 83 Janet

| • **Album sales:** 6,600,000 | • **Release date:** May 1993 |

Janet Jackson waited four long years after the release of *Rhythm Nation 1814* before bringing out what would become her biggest album to date, the simply titled *Janet,* her first album on Virgin. Long serving producers Jimmy Jam and Terry Lewis introduced a warmer sound to the album than on previous efforts, incorporating samples and a wide variety of musical styles.

Like her two previous albums, *Janet* entered the US chart at Number One, and saw Janet Jackson beat the record set by her brother Michael for first week sales, shifting 350,000 copies. The album produced seven singles in the US and six in the UK. Although Jackson had a couple of US chart toppers the most successful UK single, 'That's the Way Love Goes', peaked at Number Two.

**Number One singles:**
US: That's The Way Love Goes; Again

**Grammy awards:**
Best R&B song That's The Way Love Goes

**Label:** US & UK: Virgin

**Recorded in:** Edina, USA

**Personnel:**
Janet Jackson
Kathleen Battle
Chuck D
The Flow
Jimmy Jam
Terry Lewis
Dave Barry
Frank Stribling
David Eiland
Kenneth Holmen
Bernie Edstrom
Robert Hallgrimson
Steve Wright
Jeff Gottwig
Steven Pikal
Larry Waddell
Jimmy Wright
Mark Haynes
Stokley
Jossie Harris
Tina Landon
Ann Nesby
Jamecia Bennett
Core Cotton
Marie Graham
Jeff Taylor
Various other personnel

**Producers:**
Jimmy Jam
Terry Lewis
Janet Jackson
Jellybean Johnson

1 Morning (0:31)
2 That's The Way Love Goes (4:24)
3 You Know... (0:12)
4 You Want This (5:05)
5 Be A Good Boy (0:07)
6 If (4:31)
7 Back (0:01)
8 This Time (6:58)
9 Go On Miss Janet (0:01)
10 Throb (4:33)
11 What'll I Do (4:05)
12 The Lounge (0:15)
13 Funky Big Band (5:22)
14 Racism (0:08)
15 New Agenda (4:00)
16 Love, Pt. 2 (0:11)
17 Because Of Love (4:20)
18 Wind (0:11)
19 Again (3:46)
20 Another Lover (0:11)
21 Where Are You Now (5:47)
22 Hold On Baby (0:12)
23 The Body That Loves You (5:32)
24 Rain (0:18)
25 Anytime, Anyplace (7:08)
26 Are You Still Up (1:36)
27 Sweet Dreams (0:14)

Total album length: 70 minutes

janet.

# 82 Bat Out Of Hell II

| • **Album sales:** 6,800,000 | • **Release date:** September 1993 |

Meat Loaf, alongside producers Todd Rundgren and Jim Steinman, constructed one of rock music's defining albums in 1977's *Bat Out Of Hell*. The team had initially set out to produce a sequel to that themed epic right away, but the pressures of success took their toll on Meat Loaf in the 1980s and it seemed that the follow-up would never happen.

Meat Loaf entered something of a recovery period in the early 1990s, during which rumours abounded that he was once again working with Steinman. Sure enough the pair emerged in 1993 with the long-awaited *Bat Out Of Hell II*. The album topped the charts on both sides of the Atlantic and the single 'I'd Do Anything For Love (But I Won't Do That)' took the Number One spot in both the US and UK.

**Number One singles:** US & UK: I'd Do Anything for Love (But I Won't Do That)

**Grammy awards:** Best solo rock vocal performance – I'd Do Anything For Love (But I Won't Do That)

**Label:** US: MCA; UK: Virgin

**Recorded in:** Los Angeles & New York, USA

**Personnel:**
Meat Loaf
Mrs Loud
Jeff Bova
Tim Pierce
Eddie Martinez
Pat Thrall
Brian Meagher Sr
Brian Meagher Jr
Justin Meagher
Lenny Pickett
Roy Bittan
Bill Payne
Steve Buslowe
Kenny Aronoff
Jimmy Bralower
Rick Marotta
Kasim Sulton
Rory Dodd
Amy Goff
Elaine Goff
Jim Steinman
Cynthia Geary
Brett Cullen
Michelle Little
Robert Coron
Max Haskett
Curtis King
Todd Rundgren
Various other personnel

**Producers:**
Todd Rundgren
Jim Steinman

1 I'd Do Anything For Love (But I Won't Do That) (12:00)
2 Life is A Lemon And I Want My Money Back (8:00)
3 Rock & Roll Dreams Come Through (5:50)
4 It Just Won't Quit (7:21)
5 Out Of The Frying Pan (And Into The Fire) (7:24)
6 Objects In The Rear View Mirror May Appear Closer Than They Are (10:15)
7 Wasted Youth (2:41)
8 Everything Louder Than Everything Else (7:59)
9 Good Girls Go To Heaven (Bad Girls Go Everywhere) (6:53)
10 Back Into Hell (2:46)
11 Lost Boys and Golden Girls (4:29)

Total album length: 76 minutes

# 81 Luck Of The Draw

| • Album sales: 7,000,000 | • Release date: June 1991 |

Following the multi-Grammy winning success of *Nick Of Time*, expectations were high for Bonnie Raitt's 1991 album *Luck Of The Draw*. Raitt opted not to take her success for granted. *Nick Of Time* had emerged following a long, and ultimately successful, battle against the booze, and Raitt wished to ensure that the critical acclaim and commercial success were deserved.

After a period of creative retreat, Raitt again teamed up with *Nick Of Time* producer Don Was for an effort that not only built upon, but eclipsed that album's success. As the long years of hard work finally began to pay of – Raitt had been a recording artist since 1971 – so Raitt's confidence in her own songwriting abilities grew.

One of the most poignant songs included, 'One Part Be My Lover', was based on a poem left on Raitt's pillow by her boyfriend, actor Michael O'Keefe, following an argument. Three other songs were penned entirely by Raitt, more than on any previous collection.

**Number One Singles:**
None

**Grammy awards:**
Best female pop vocal performance – Something To Talk About; Best solo rock vocal performance – Luck Of The Draw; Best rock performance by a duo or group with vocal – Good Man, Good Woman

**Label:** US & UK: Capitol

**Recorded in:**
Los Angeles, USA

**Personnel:**
Bonnie Raitt
Stephen Bruton
Mark Goldenberg
Randy Jacobs

Robben Ford
Scott Thurston
Billy Vera
Ivan Neville
Ian McLagan
Benmont Tench
Steve Conn
James 'Hutch Hutchinson
Don Was
Ricky Fataar
Curt Bisquera
Tony Braunagel
Jeff Porcaro
Debra Dobkin
Paulinho DaCosta
Sweet Pea Atkinson
Sir Harry Bowens
Kris Kristofferson
Various other personnel

**Producers:**
Bonnie Raitt
Don Was

1 **Something to Talk About** (3:47)
2 **Good Man, Good Woman** (3:33)
3 **I Can't Make You Love Me** (5:33)
4 **Tangled And Dark** (4:52)
5 **Come To Me** (4:20)
6 **No Business** (4:24)
7 **One Part Be My Lover** (5:06)
8 **Not The Only One** (5:03)
9 **Papa Come Quick (Jody And Chico)** (2:43)
10 **Slow Ride** (3:59)
11 **Luck Of The Draw** (5:17)
12 **All At Once** (5:03)

Total album length: 53 minutes

LUCK of
BONNIE
RAITT
the DRAW

# 80 Waiting To Exhale

| • **Album sales:** 7,000,000 | • **Release date:** November 1995 |

**B**ucking the trend for the painting-by-numbers soundtracks that had continued to dominate the record shops since *Flashdance* defined the form in 1983, *Waiting To Exhale* is as much a Babyface album and showcase for some of America's top divas, as it is a soundtrack.

Babyface and Whitney Houston had collaborated before on the multi-Grammy winning soundtrack to *The Bodyguard*, and the pressure was on for a similarly sized hit production. Of the 16 tracks on *Waiting To Exhale*, 15 are original compositions written or co-written by Babyface, the sole cover version being a smoky rendering of 'My Funny Valentine' by Chaka Khan. Although Whitney Houston, one of the stars of the weepy Forest Whitaker-directed film, only contributed vocals to three tracks, she certainly contributed to the album's success. Her recording of 'Exhale' topped the US singles chart. Other talent on the album ranges from Mary J Blige to Aretha Franklin.

*Waiting To Exhale* reached Number One on the Billboard Top 200.

**Number One Singles:**
None

**Grammy awards:**
Best R&B song – Exhale
(Shoop, Shoop)

**Label:** US & UK: Arista

**Recorded in:**
Various locations

**Personnel:**
Whitney Houston
Aretha Franklin

Toni Braxton
Chaka Khan
Patti Labelle
Chante Moore
Tionne 'T-Boz' Watkins
Lisa 'Left Eye' Lopes
Rozonda 'Chilli' Thomas
Mary J Blige
Brandy
Faith Evans
CeCe Winans
Various other personnel

**Producer:**
Babyface

1 Exhale (Shoop, Shoop)
(Whitney Houston) (3:24)
2 Why Does It Hurt So Bad
(Whitney Houston) (4:37)
3 Let It Flow (Toni Braxton)
(4:27)
4 It Hurts Like Hell
(Aretha Franklin) (4:19)
5 Sittin' Up In My Room
(Brandy) (4:52)
6 This Is How It Works
(TLC) (5:00)
7 Not Gon' Cry
(Mary J Blige) (4:57)
8 My Funny Valentine
(Chaka Khan) (4:06)
9 And I Gave My Love to

You (Sonja Marie) (4:48)
10 All Night Long (SWV)
(4:31)
11 Wey U (Chanté Moore)
(4:32)
12 My Love, Sweet Love
(Patti LaBelle) (4:21)
13 Kissing You
(Faith Evans) (3:23)
14 Love Will Be Waiting at
Home (For Real) (5:59)
15 How Could You Call Her
Baby (Shanna) (5:09)
16 Count On Me
(Whitney Houston) (4:26)

Total album length: 73 minutes

# Waiting to Exhale

## Original Soundtrack Album

**Includes new music by**
Whitney Houston, Mary J. Blige, Brandy, Toni Braxton, Faith Evans,
Aretha Franklin, Chaka Khan, Patti LaBelle, Chanté Moore,
For Real, SWV, Shanna, Sonja Marie, TLC and CeCe Winans.
**All New Songs Written and Produced by Babyface**

# 79 Crash

| • Album sales: 7,000,000 | • Release date: April 1996 |

Following the enormous success of their first major label release, *Under The Table and Dreaming*, Dave Matthews Band found themselves with a ready supply of new songs that had been honed to perfection during an extensive tour. Rather than rest on their laurels, the band decided to release *Crash*. They retained noted producer Steve Lillywhite, who had helped polish their live sound into a hit studio album. However, after the strong sales of *Under the Table and Dreaming*, the band were confident enough to strive for a looser, less formal sound.

The single 'Crash Into Me' became a huge radio hit, and was one of only two genuinely new songs recorded for the album. All the other tracks had already been performed many times during the band's recent tour. One of the older tracks was 'Tripping Billies', first recorded on the band's *Remember Two Things*, a self-produced album recorded live and issued in 1993. Additional singles, 'Too Much' and 'So Much To Say', continued the band's crossover success on radio and MTV, while the album was nominated for a Grammy for Best Rock Album.

*Crash* debuted and peaked at Number Two on the Billboard Top 200, quickly reaching platinum status. The band continued to tour throughout 1996 and propelled the album to double platinum status by November of that year.

**Number One singles:**
None

**Grammy awards:** Best rock vocal performance by a duo or group

**Label:** US & UK: RCA

**Recorded in:**
Bearsville, USA

**Personnel:**
David Matthews
Boyd Tinsley
Leroi Moore
Stefan Lessard
Carter Beauford
Tim Reynolds

**Producer:**
Steve Lillywhite

1   So Much To Say  (4:07)
2   Two Step  (6:27)
3   Crash Into Me  (5:16)
4   Too Much  (4:21)
5   #41  (6:39)
6   Say Goodbye  (6:11)
7   Drive In Drive Out  (5:54)
8   Let You Down  (4:07)
9   Lie In Our Graves  (5:42)
10  Cry Freedom  (5:53)
11  Tripping Billies  (5:00)
12  Proudest Monkey  (9:11)

Total album length: 69 minutes

Dave Matthews Band

crash

# 78 *N Sync

• **Album sales:** 7,000,000 | • **Release date:** March 1998

Taking few chances with their bid for US fame and fortune, *N Sync recruited manager Lou Pearlman from their hometown of Orlando, Florida. The band signed an initial record deal with BMG Ariola, Munich, and their debut album, *N Sync*, received its first release in Europe, with the singles 'I Want You Back' and 'Tearin' Up My Heart' becoming huge hits across the continent.

The US release of *N Sync* followed in spring of 1998, after the band had spent a year touring and building their careers in Europe and Asia. Still virtual unknowns in the US, the quintet supported the album with a series of live appearances at roller-skating rinks across the country. This effort paid off when the single 'I Want You Back' made it to Number 13 on the Billboard Top 100.

To ensure their music could be crafted into a suitable pop style aimed squarely at teenagers, *N Sync drafted several producers, including Backstreet Boys producer Kristian Lundin. Denniz Pop and Max Martin, who had worked with Ace Of Base were also brought on board. The album peaked at number 2 in the Billboard Top 200 and Number 30 in the UK.

**Number One singles:**
None

**Grammy awards:** None.

**Label:** US: RCA;
UK: Arista

**Recorded in:** N/A

**Personnel:**
Lance Bass
Joey Fatone
Chris Kirkpatrick
Justin Timberlake
J C Chasez
Carl Sturken

Veit Renn
Tony Battaglia
Mark Matteo
Elizabeth Chang
Alexander Yudkovsky
Maxine Neuman
Daniel Miller
Jolyon Skinner
Full Force

**Producers:**
Full Force
Veit Renn
Denniz Pop
Max Martin
Kristian Lundin

1 Tearin' Up My Heart (3:30)
2 I Just Wanna Be With You (4:30)
3 Here We Go (3:35)
4 For The Girl Who Has Everything (3:45)
5 God Must Have Spent A Little More Time On You (4:42)
6 You Got It (3:33)
7 I Need Love (3:14)
8 I Want You Back (3:21)
9 Everything I Own (3:57)
10 I Drive Myself Crazy (4:00)
11 Crazy For You (3:40)
12 Sailing (4:38)
13 Giddy Up (4:08)

Total album length: 50 minutes

# 77 August And Everything After

| • **Album sales:** 7,100,000 | • **Release date:** February 1993 |

Counting Crows recorded their debut album in early 1993 at a rented house in Hollywood. The release of the album later that year provoked comparisons to The Band and Van Morrison, offering a popular alternative to the plethora of grunge rock then dominating the rock scene.

*August And Everything After* showcased the band's richly crafted brand of harmonic rock and the dexterity of singer Adam Duritz's rousing voice. The album's centrepiece, the radio-friendly single 'Mr Jones', proved a major hit and helped to drive the album to Number Four in the Billboard Top 200 album chart. It remained on the chart for a total of 93 weeks.

With renowned producer T-Bone Burnett working his magic in the studio, the band mixed driving anthems with evocative ballads, while injecting a rural country-rock edge. A dark often morose record, Duritz's expressive voice lends an intimate atmosphere to cuts like of 'Anna Begins' and 'Rain King'. Bar the guitar-jangle of 'Mr Jones', there was little else in the way of single fodder, but amid a wealth of critical acclaim the band toured the album for over a year.

**Number One singles:**
None

**Grammy awards:** None

**Label:** US & UK: Geffen

**Recorded in:**
Hollywood, USA

**Personnel:**
Matt Malley
David Bryson
Charlie Gillingham
Adam Duritz
Steve Bowman
David Immergluck
Bill Dillon
T-Bone Burnett
Denny Fongheiser
Maria McKee
Gary Louris,
Mark Olson

**Producer:**
T-Bone Burnett

1 **Round Here** (5:32)
2 **Omaha** (3:40)
3 **Mr Jones** (4:33)
4 **Perfect Blue Buildings** (5:01)
5 **Anna Begins** (4:32)
6 **Time And Time Again** (5:13)
7 **Rain King** (4:16)
8 **Sullivan Street** (4:29)
9 **Ghost Train** (4:01)
10 **Raining In Baltimore** (4:41)
11 **A Murder Of One** (5:44)

Total album length: 51 minutes

They're waking up Maria 'cause everybodyelse has got
She makes a little motion with her head                    Rol
And says she's gonna st     for a couple minute
I     said "                           ana       the cold hea
I've  say  I'm sorry, by now, at    once to
She says: "I've forgotten what I'm supposed to
And it slips my                              s  suppo
I'm getting older and   der and older
And always a little further out of the w

# Counting Crows

You look into her eyes and    it's more than you he
In August and Everything        You get a lit

## August and Everything After

I stumbled into Washington Square just as the sun
I walked across the lawn to the cathedral

# 76 Vs.

| • Album sales: 7,100,000 | • Release date: October 1993 |

Pearl Jam's debut album, *Ten*, had helped unleash the grunge scene alongside Nirvana's *Nevermind*, which it ultimately outsold. However, Eddie Vedder was wary of Pearl Jam becoming too commercialized and refused to film any videos to support the follow up album, *Vs*. Press access was restricted, and a supporting tour was scaled down, partly due to a perceived Ticketmaster monopoly over ticketing for live events. It was Vedder's rallying cry against the corporate conventions of the industry that would define the shift from *Ten* to the appropriately titled *Vs*. (a title which appears nowhere on the sleeve). The album also sees a rawer, less structured sound emerge.

Pearl Jam had toured extensively prior to recording *Vs.*, and the experience enabled the band to record the album as one live take, playing the tracks through over several days before picking the best recording for the final album.

Despite the band's anti-corporate stance *Vs*. debuted at Number One, after being released a week earlier on vinyl only, and sold nearly a million copies during the first week of general release. *Vs*. peaked at Number Two in the UK, the band's highest position to date.

| | |
|---|---|
| **Number One Singles:** None | **Personnel:** Eddie Vedder |
| | Stone Gossard |
| **Grammy awards:** None | Mike McCready |
| | Jeff Ament |
| **Label:** US & UK: Epic | Dave Abbruzzese |
| **Recorded in:** Nicasio & Seattle, USA | **Producers:** Brendan O'Brien |
| | Eddie Vedder |
| | Stone Gossard |
| | Mike McCready |
| | Jeff Ament |
| | Dave Abbruzzese |

1  Go (3:13)
2  Animal (2:49)
3  Daughter (3:56)
4  Glorified G (3:26)
5  Dissident (3:36)
6  W M A (5:59)
7  Blood (2:51)
8  Rear View Mirror (4:44)
9  Rats (4:15)
10 Elderly Woman Behind the Counter in a Small Town (3:16)
11 Leash (3:09)
12 Indifference (5:06)

Total album length: 46 minutes

# 75 Hell Freezes Over

| • **Album sales:** 7,100,000 | • **Release date:** November 1994 |

The Eagles' *Hell Freezes Over* marked their first new album in 14 years, with four newly written tracks leading into a live collection of material recorded during an MTV concert special.

The new studio material includes two collaborations with Don Henley, the surprisingly emotive 'Learn To Be Still' and the Top 40 hit 'Get Over It'. The tender ballad 'Love Will Keep Us Alive' and country lilt of 'The Girl From Yesterday' complete the new studio work while the remainder of the live, mostly acoustic, album finds Frey, Henley, Walsh, Schmit, and Felder delivering meticulous renditions of Eagles classics, such as 'Hotel California', 'Take It Easy', and 'Life In The Fast Lane'. Concentrating on the latter part of their career, *Hell Freezes Over* is awash with elements of blues, R&B, country and polished harmonic rock, which propelled the album to Number One on the Billboard chart.

To support the album, the band undertook a mammoth US tour that ran up to August 1996.

**Number One singles:**
None

**Grammy awards:** None

**Label:** US & UK: Geffen

**Recorded in:**
Los Angeles, USA;
Toronto, Canada

**Personnel:**
Don Felder
Glenn Frey
Joe Walsh
Timothy B Schmit
Don Henley

John Corey
Timothy Drury
Jay Oliver
Scott Crago
Gary Grimm
Stan Lynch
Paulinho Da Costa

**Producers:**
Elliot Scheiner
Rob Jacobs
Stan Lynch
Don Felder
Glenn Frey
Joe Walsh
Timothy B Schmit
Don Henley

1 Get Over It (3:29)
2 Love Will Keep Us Alive (4:00)
3 The Girl From Yesterday (3:21)
4 Learn To Be Still (4:27)
5 Tequila Sunrise (2:56)
6 Hotel California (6:54)
7 Wasted Time (5:03)
8 Pretty Maids All In A Row (4:15)
9 I Can't Tell You Why (5:11)
10 New York Minute (6:37)
11 The Last Resort (7:24)
12 Take It Easy (4:36)
13 In The City (4:07)
14 Life In the Fast Lane (6:01)
15 Desperado (4:15)

Total album length: 72 minutes

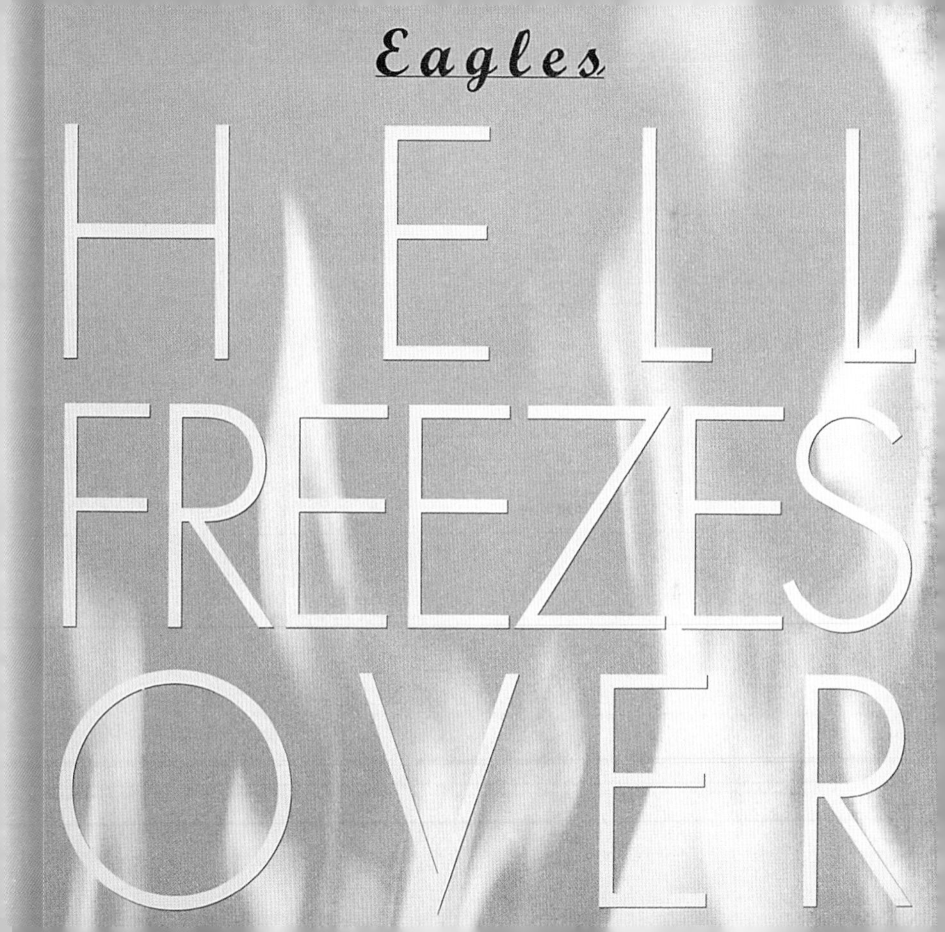
Eagles
HELL
FREEZES
OVER

# 74 No Way Out

| • **Album sales:** 7,100,000 | • **Release date:** July 1997 |

*No Way Out* marked the start of a successful recording career for Puff Daddy, aka Sean 'Puffy' Combs, following his work as a dancer, producer and record executive. Released shortly after the fatal shooting of his friend and colleague the Notorious B.I.G., Combs' debut is weighed down with a sense of loss and frustration – yet proved an enormous global success.

Recorded in the Caribbean Sound Basin, Trinidad and the US, the release of *No Way Out* was delayed for several months as Combs grieved his friend. While the sense of loss gives *No Way Out* substance, a significant dose of party tunes prevent it form being too morose.

The combination propelled *No Way Out* to the top of the charts. The first single 'Can't Nobody Hold Me Down' held on to the peak of the US singles charts for almost two months and reached Number 19 in the UK. It was followed by the poignant tribute 'I'll Be Missing You', mixing the music of the Police's 'Every Breath You Take' with Faith Evans' vocals.

**Number One singles:**
US & UK: I'll Be Missing You; US: Can't Nobody Hold Me Down

**Grammy awards:**
Best rap album

**Label:** US: Bad Boy
UK: Arista

**Recorded in:**
Trinidad; Atlanta & New York, USA

**Personnel:**
Puff Daddy
Carl Thomas
Faith Evans
112

Ginuwine
The Notorious B.I.G
Lil' Kim
Foxy Brown
The Lox
Mase
Black Rob
Busta Rhymes
Jay-Z
Twista
Melissa Feliciano
Stevie J
Various other personnel

**Producers:**
Stevie J
Puff Combs
Ron Lawrence
Deric 'D-Dot' Angelettie
Carlos Broady

1  No Way Out (1:22)
2  Victory (4:56)
3  Been Around The World (5:25)
4  What You Gonna Do? (4:55)
5  Don't Stop What You're Doing (3:58)
6  If I Should Die Tonight (2:59)
7  Do You Know (6:06)
8  Young G's (5:25)
9  I Love You Baby (4:03)
10 It's All About The Benjamins (4:38)
11 Pain (5:08)
12 Is This The End? (4:34)
13 I Got The Power (4:05)
14 Friend (6:37)
15 Señorita (4:07)
16 I'll Be Missing You (5:43)
17 Can't Nobody Hold Me Down (3:51)

Total album length: 74 minutes

# 73 Sevens

| • **Album sales:** 7,100,000 | • **Release date:** November 1997 |

For his seventh album, Garth Brooks returned to the country music genre he had dominated prior to his rock-influenced *Fresh Horses*. That ill-advised attempt to launch into the arena rock scene had produced relatively lacklustre sales and on *Sevens* Brooks' attempted to recapture his original fan base with return to more traditional country. But Brooks still managed to broaden his musical horizons by drawing on writing partners outside the Nashville mainstream, such as Pierce Bettis and Joe Henry.

During its first day on sale *Sevens* sold 375,000 copies, a massive figure for a country album. With 12 of the 14 tracks of the album charting on the Billboard Hot Country Singles & Tracks chart, Brooks managed to beat his own record for the most tracks from one album appearing on one chart – a record held previously by eight singles from *Fresh Horses*.

**Number One Singles:**
None

**Grammy awards:**
Country collaboration with vocals – In Another's Eyes

**Label:** US & UK: Capitol

**Recorded in:**
Nashville, USA

**Personnel:**
Garth Brooks
Trisha Yearwood
Steve Wariner
Shawn Camp
Carl Jackson
Chris Leuzinger
Mark Casstevens
Pat Flynn
Bruce Bouton
Al Perkins
Rob Hajacos
Randy Howard
Bobby Wood
Catherine Styron
Mike Chapman
Kevin Grant
Milton Sledge
Randy Hardison
Sam Bacco
Susan Ashton
Kathy Chiavola
Vicki Hampton
Robert Bailey
Yvonne Hodges
Dorothy Robinson
Charles Green
Matt Lindsey
Sandy Mason
Big Al
Double 'D'
'Sam the Man' Duczer
Leona Heid

**Producers:**
Allen Reynolds
Denise Jarvis

1 Longneck Bottle (2:17)
2 How You Ever Gonna Know (3:36)
3 She's Gonna Make It (2:47)
4 I Don't Have To Wonder (3:04)
5 Two Piña Coladas (3:35)
6 Cowboy Cadillac (2:51)
7 Fit For A King (4:06)
8 Do What You Gotta Do (2:59)
9 You Move Me (4:34)
10 In Another's Eyes (3:33)
11 When There's No One Around (3:33)
12 Friend To Me (3:02)
13 Take The Keys To My Heart (2:32)
14 Belleau Wood (3:29)

Total album length: 46 minutes

SEVENS

# 72 Significant Other

| • Album sales: 7,100,000 | • Release date: June 1999 |

Limp Bizkit secured their reputation as purveyors of a new brand of hip-hop-influenced rock with the release of their second album *Significant Other*. As if to confirm their arrival as a major new name, the album was also released in an edited, family-friendly version.

A heavy touring schedule had helped to refine the band's distinctive sound, while Fred Durst's songwriting talents had matured in the two years since their debut. The first single, 'Nookie', the track most reminiscent of early Limp Bizkit, somewhat belied the evolution of the band. Nevertheless, Durst's self-directed video for the single played a major part in elevating the band to superstar status.

The writing of the album coincided with Durst splitting up with his long-time girlfriend, with 'Nookie' presenting a particularly brutal indictment of the demise of their relationship. Durst's other, rather more casual, dalliances with members of the opposite sex, also inform his lyrics, most notably 'No Sex'. The album definitely wears its hip-hop colours on its sleeve with the hiring of House Of Pain's DJ Lethal on turntables, and appearances by noteworthy artists including Method Man and DJ Premier.

**Number One Singles:**
None

**Grammy awards:** None

**Label:** US & UK: Interscope

**Recorded in:** North Hollywood, USA

**Personnel:**
Fred Durst
Wes Borland
Sam Rivers
John Otto
DJ Lethal
Method Man
Les Claypool

Matt Pinfield
Anita Durst
Mathematics
Scott Borland
Jonathan Davis
Aaron Lewis
Eve Butler
Various other personnel

**Producers:**
Scott Weiland
Terry Date
D.J. Premier
Fred Durst
Wes Borland
Sam Rivers
John Otto
DJ Lethal

1   Intro  (0:37)
2   Just Like This  (3:35)
3   Nookie  (4:50)
4   Break Stuff  (2:47)
5   Re-Arranged  (5:54)
6   I'm Broke  (4:00)
7   Nobody Like You  (4:20)
8   Don't Go Off Wandering  (4:00)
9   9 Teen 90 Nine  (4:36)
10  N 2 Gether Now  (4:50)
11  Trust?  (4:59)
12  No Sex  (3:54)
13  Show Me What You Got  (4:27)
14  Lesson Learned  (2:40)
15  Outro  (7:24)

Total album length: 63 minutes

# 71 The Score

| • **Album sales:** 7,200,000 | • **Release date:** February 1996 |

The Fugee's breakthrough album showcased the eclectic tastes of all three MCs – Lauryn Hill, Pras and Wyclef – while offering an incredibly popular alternative to the macho-posturing of the gangster rap that dominated the mid-1990s. Innovative and derivative in equal measure, *The Score* blends the work of Roberta Flack and Bob Marley with cinematic constraints and a social conscience. The group served up a fascinating mixture of soul, reggae, gospel and blues, all within the framework of inventive hip-hop.

It was the group's treatment of 'Killing Me Softly' and Hill's moving vocal on 'Ready or Not' that drove *The Score* to multi-platinum success. Released as singles, the former topped the UK chart for five weeks, followed by a three week stint by 'Ready Or Not'. While the singles failed to hit the Top 40 in the US, *The Score* stayed at the top of the Billboard chart for four weeks.

**Number One singles:** UK: Killing Me Softly; Ready or Not

**Grammy awards:** Best rap album; Best R&B performance by a duo or group – Killing Me Softly With His Song

**Label:** US: Ruffhouse UK: Columbia

**Recorded in:** New Jersey & New York, USA; Kingston, Jamaica

**Personnel:** Lauryn Hill Prakazrel 'Pras'

Wyclef Jean
Garfield 'Gus' Parkinson
Red Alert
Ras Baraka
Handel Tucker
Robbie Shakespeare
Sly Dunbar
Forte
Omega
Diamond D
Pace 1
Young Zee
Ra Digga

**Producers:**
Wyclef
Shawn King
Lauryn Hill
Salaam Remi
John Forte

1   **Red Intro** (1:51)
2   **How Many Mics** (4:28)
3   **Ready Or Not** (3:47)
4   **Zealots** (4:20)
5   **The Beast** (5:37)
6   **Fu-Gee-La** (4:20)
7   **Family Business** (5:43)
8   **Killing Me Softly With His Song** (4:58)
9   **The Score** (5:02)
10  **The Mask** (4:50)
11  **Cowboys** (5:23)
12  **No Woman, No Cry** (4:33)
13  **Manifest/Outro** (5:59)
14  **Fu-Gee-La** (4:24)
15  **Fu-Gee-La** (5:27)

Total album length: 67 minutes

# 70 To The Extreme

| • **Album sales:** 7,300,000 | • **Release date:** August 1990 |

A huge international hit, *To the Extreme* showed that a white rapper could become a mainstream success. Robert Van Winkle, aka Vanilla Ice, took the chart by storm with his debut album selling over 7,000,000 copies before bogus claims about his violent past just as swiftly sparked his downfall.

Controversy raged around the rapper who not only mirrored MC Hammer's rapping style, but attempted to deny obvious rock and pop references such as David Bowie and Queen's 'Under Pressure' and the Rolling Stones' 'Satisfaction'. Ice's transformation of the former track into the single 'Ice Ice Baby' proved enormously profitable. Released as a single, it topped the charts in the US and UK and sold 15,000,000 copies worldwide. Subsequently, his televised denial that he ripped off 'Under Pressure' was voted the 12th Most Outrageous Moment on MTV.

*To the Extreme* casts the net wide, incorporating dance, mid-tempo ballads and even an attempt at gangster rap with 'Go III'. The album hit the peak of the Billboard Top 200 chart in the US and became the first album to reach all five certification levels – gold, platinum, double-platinum, triple-platinum and quadruple-platinum – in only a month. It spent a total of 16 weeks in the top spot, longer than the 1991 follow-up, *Cool as Ice*, spent in the Top 200.

**Number One singles:**
US & UK: Ice Ice Baby

**Grammy awards:** None

**Label:** US: Alliance;
UK: SBK

**Recorded in:** N/A

**Personnel:**
Vanilla Ice
Deshay
Paul Loomis
Craig Pride

**Producers:**
Vanilla Ice
Darryl Williams
Khayree
Kim Sharp
Tommy Quon
Paul Loomis

1   Ice Ice Baby (4:31)
2   Yo Vanilla (0:04)
3   Stop That Train (4:29)
4   Hooked (4:52)
5   Ice Is Workin' It (4:36)
6   Life Is A Fantasy (4:47)
7   Play That Funky Music (4:22)
8   Dancin' (5:00)
9   Go III (4:58)
10  It's A Party (4:39)
11  Juice To Get Loose Boy (0:08)
12  Ice Cold (4:05)
13  Rosta Man (4:36)
14  I Love You (5:06)
15  Havin' A Roni (1:09)

Total album length: 57 minutes

**Vanilla Ice**

VANILLA ICE
TO THE EXTREME

Sleeve artwork by Janet Perr and Michael Levine

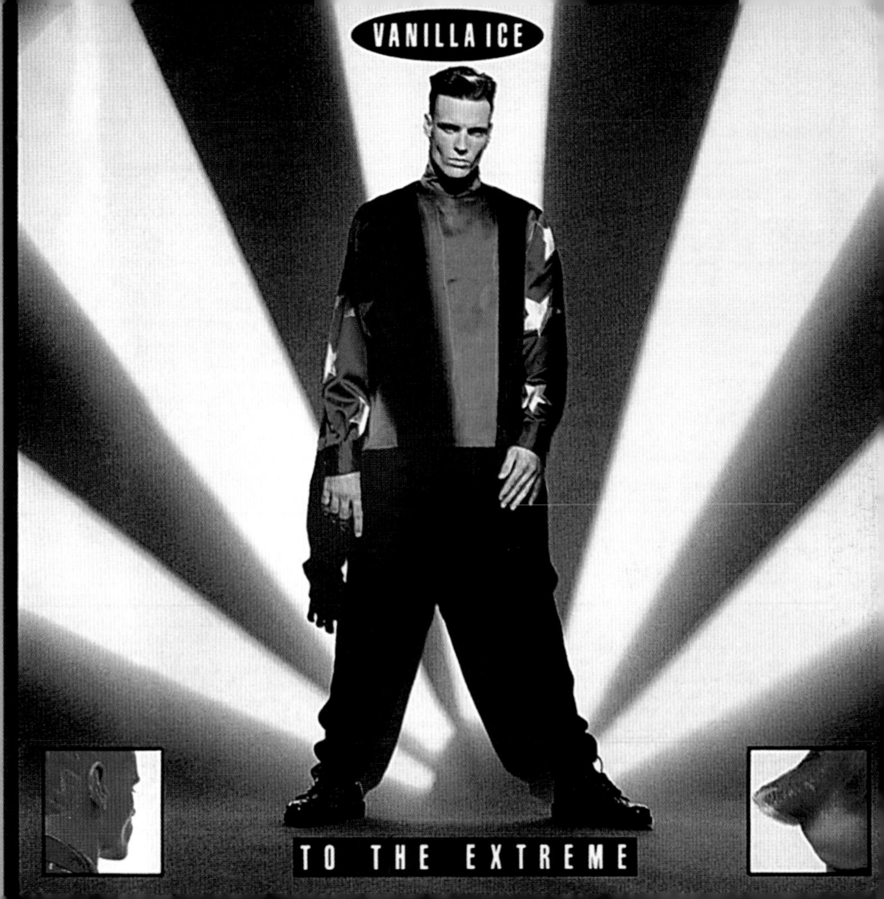

# 69 Use Your Illusion I & II

**• Album sales:** 7,300,000 **| • Release date:** September 1991 |

Having rocketed in to the public eye with their raucous debut album *Appetite For Destruction,* Guns N' Roses kept their legions of fans waiting three years for the next album proper, before unleashing two simultaneously. Showcasing a more bombastic sound, the albums marked a considerable departure from their guttural blues-based roots.

*Use Your Illusion I* and *II* were delayed due to internal wranglings and personal problems, a tumultuous time that saw drummer Steve Adler

sacked and replaced by former Cult drummer Matt Sorum. Stacked full of epic ballads utilizing strings and piano, the new sound proved popular with fans, but sparked disarray within the group, leading to the departure of guitarist Izzy Stradlin barely two months after release.

The *Use Your Illusion* albums debuted in the top two spots on the US Billboard Top 200 and reached Number One and Number Two in the UK.

| **Number One singles:** | **Personnel:** |
|---|---|
| None | Izzy Stradlin |
| | Axl Rose |
| **Grammy awards:** None | Slash |
| | Duff McKagan |
| **Label:** US & UK: Geffen | Dizzy Reed |
| | Matt Sorum |
| **Recorded in:** | |
| Hollywood & Los Angeles, USA; Toronto, Canada | **Producers:** |
| | Izzy Stradlin |
| | Axl Rose |
| | Slash |
| | Duff McKagan |
| | Dizzy Reed |
| | Matt Sorum |
| | Mike Clink |

**Volume 1**
1 Right Next Door To Hell (3:02)
2 Dust N' Bones (4:59)
3 Live And Let Die (3:03)
4 Don't Cry (4:44)
5 Perfect Crime (2:23)
6 You Ain't The First (2:37)
7 Bad Obsession (5:28)
8 Back Off Bitch (5:04)
9 Double Talkin' Jive (3:22)
10 November Rain (8:59)
11 The Garden (5:21)
12 Garden Of Eden (2:41)
13 Don't Damn Me (5:19)
14 Bad Apples (4:28)
15 Dead Horse (4:18)
16 Coma (10:16)

**Volume 2**
1 Civil War (7:36)
2 14 Years (4:17)
3 Yesterdays (3:13)
4 Knockin' On Heaven's Door (5:36)
5 Get In The Ring (5:29)
6 Shotgun Blues (3:23)
7 Breakdown (6:58)
8 Pretty Tied Up (The Perils Of Rock & Roll Decadence) (4:46)
9 Locomotive (8:42)
10 So Fine (4:09)
11 Estranged (9:20)
12 You Could Be Mine (5:48)
13 Don't Cry (4:42)
14 My World (1:22)

Combined album length 151 minutes

# 68 Blood Sugar Sex Magik

| • **Album sales:** 7,300,000 | • **Release date:** September 1991 |

Recorded in a Los Angeles mansion in 1990, not long after the death of founding guitarist Hillel Slovak, a troubled Red Hot Chili Peppers teamed up with renowned Beastie Boys producer Rick Rubin to record one of the seminal albums of the 1990s. Their fifth album, *Blood Sugar Sex Magik* mixed rock guitars and pounding funk-fuelled baselines with a hip-hop swagger and punk sensibility. It proved the band's breakthrough, while influencing a myriad of artists from Dr Dre to Limp Bizkit.

Central to the assured feel of the album are singer Anthony Kiedis' typically sexually-charged and explicit lyrics, which cover everything from failed relationships (in 'I Could Have Lied' and 'Breaking The Girl'), to his own drug addiction (in the emotive ballad 'Under The Bridge'). His soaring rap-edged vocal moves up a gear for the infectious funk-rockers 'Give It Away' and 'The Power Of Equality', while all 17 gems come underpinned by Flea's irresistible, surging bass.

*Blood Sugar Sex Magik* peaked at Number Three in the US, while reaching Number 25 in the UK. The album spawned a string of hit singles, including 'Under The Bridge' which made Number Two on the Billboard Hot 100. The single 'Give It Away' won Best Hard Rock Performance With Vocal at 1992's Grammy Awards.

**Number One singles:**
None

**Grammy awards:** Best hard rock performance with vocal

**Label:** US & UK: Warner

**Recorded in:**
Los Angeles, USA

**Personnel:**
Anthony Kiedis
Flea
John Frusciante
Chad Smith
Dave Navarro

**Producer:**
Rick Rubin

1 The Power Of Equality (4:03)
2 If You Have To Ask (3:37)
3 Breaking The Girl (4:55)
4 Funky Monks (5:23)
5 Suck My Kiss (3:37)
6 I Could Have Lied (4:04)
7 Mellowship Slinky In B Major (4:00)
8 The Righteous And The Wicked (4:08)
9 Give It Away (4:43)
10 Blood Sugar Sex Magik (4:31)
11 Under The Bridge (4:24)
12 Naked In The Rain (4:26)
13 Apache Rose Peacock (4:42)
14 The Greeting Song (3:14)
15 My Lovely Man (4:39)
16 Sir Psycho Sexy (8:17)
17 They're Red Hot (1:12)

Total album length: 73 minutes

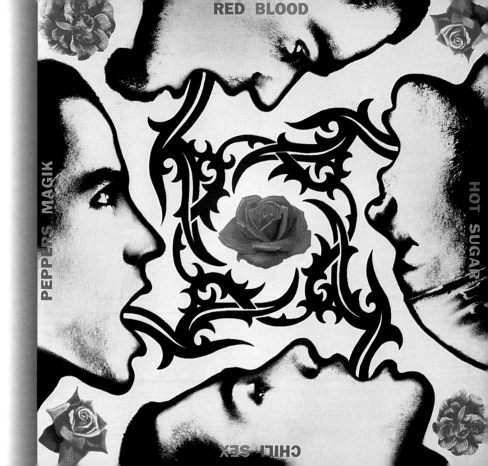

# 67 Ricky Martin

| • **Album sales:** 7,300,000 | • **Release date:** May 1999 |

Already a star in Latin America due to his tenure in boy-band Menudo and a successful solo career, Puerto Rican-born Ricky Martin stepped into the international limelight for the first time with his English-language debut.

**Number One singles:** US & UK: Livin' La Vida Loca

**Grammy awards:** None

**Label:** US: Sony; UK: Columbia

**Recorded in:** N/A

**Personnel:**
Ricky Martin
Madonna
Meja
Robi Rova
Dan Warner
Eric Bazilian
Tommy Anthony
William Orbit
Manny Lopez
Rusty Anderson
Rene Toledo
Tony Concepcion
Randall Barlow
Paquito Hechavarria
Randy Cantor
Rob Hyman
Ricardo Suarez
Hugh McDonald
Kenny Aronoff
Alex Saris
Lee Levin
Luis Enrique
Rafael Solano
Jon Secada
Gyan
Sueann Carwell

**Producers:**
Desmond Child
Robi Rosa
Madonn
William Orbit
Jon Secada
Walter Afanasieff

The first single, 'Livin' La Vida Loca' peaked at Number One on both sides of the Atlantic, while the equally infectious follow-up 'She's All I Ever Had' peaked at Number Two in the US. Along with a cameo from Swedish singer Meja on 'Private Emotion', *Ricky Martin* finds the singer sharing the microphone with Madonna on the duet 'Be Careful (Cuidado Con Mi Corazon)'.

Reportedly two years in the making, the album peaked at Number One on the Billboard Top 200, before going on to win legendary producer Walter Afanasieff a Grammy award for Producer of the Year. The same year 'Livin' La Vida Loca' won the 2000 Billboard Latin Music Award for Latin Pop Track of the Year.

1 Livin' La Vida Loca (4:03)
2 Spanish Eyes (4:05)
3 She's All I Ever Had (4:55)
4 Shake Your Bon-Bon (3:12)
5 Be Careful (Cuidadi Con Mi Corazon) (4:04)
6 I Am Made Of You (4:39)
7 Love You For A Day (3:46)
8 Private Emotion (4:02)
9 The Cup Of Life (4:39)
10 You Stay With Me (4:12)
11 Livin' La Vida Loca (4:04)
12 I Count The Minutes (4:18)
13 Bella (She's All I Ever Had) (4:56)
14 Maria (7:06)

Total album length: 60 minutes

# RICKY MARTIN

# 66 The Colour Of My Love

| • Album sales: 7,500,000 | • Release date: November 1993 |

Released by the Canadian singer following a tour with Michael Bolton, *The Colour Of My Love* was a career-defining album for Celine Dion. The album is packed full of radio-friendly tracks such as 'Only One Road' and 'Misled' and provided Dion with her first chart-topping single in the US, 'The Power Of Love', a cover of Jennifer Rush's 1985 hit.

Dion benefited from some Hollywood-fuelled exposure when the first single 'When I Fall in Love' appeared on the *Sleepless In Seattle* soundtrack, while its successor 'Because You Loved Me,' featured in promotions for Robert Redford's *Up Close and Personal*.

But it was 'The Power Of Love' that was the album's biggest hit, spending four weeks atop the Billboard Hot 100. 'Think Twice' spent several weeks at the peak of the singles chart in the UK, before charting strongly in the US.

**Number One singles:**
US: The Power of Love;
UK: Think Twice

**Grammy awards:** None

**Label:** US & UK: Epic

**Recorded In:** N/A

**Personnel:**
Celine Dion
Aldo Nova
Bob Mann
Tim Renwick
Michael Thompson
Dean Parks
Peter Zizzo
Andre Proulx
David Foster

Walter Afanasieff
Guy Roche
Russ Desalvo
John Pierce
Jimmy Greco
Jimmy Bralower
Steve Piggo
Lenny Castro
Simond Franglen
Maria Christensen
Lajuan Carter
Eddie Stockley
Earl Robinson

**Producers:**
Walter Afanasieff
David Foster
Ric Wake
Christopher Neil
Guy Roche

1 The Power Of Love (5:43)
2 Misled (3:31)
3 Think Twice (4:48)
4 Only One Road (4:49)
5 Everybody's Talkin' My Baby Down (4:02)
6 Next Plane Out (4:59)
7 Real Emotion (4:26)
8 When I Fall In Love (4:20)
9 Love Doesn't Ask Why (4:08)
10 Refuse To Dance (4:21)
11 I Remember L A (4:13)
12 No Living Without Loving You (4:23)
13 Lovin' Proof (4:12)
14 The Colour Of My Love (3:25)

Total album length: 58 minutes

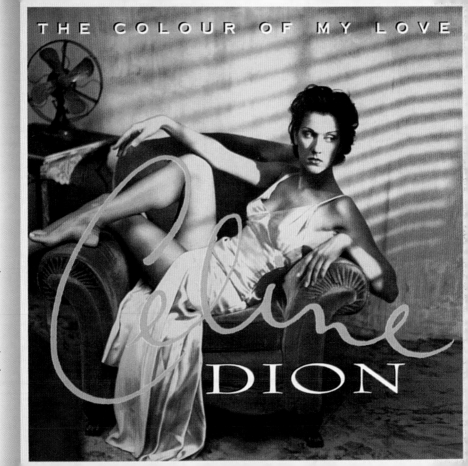

THE COLOUR OF MY LOVE

Celine
DION

# 65 Tuesday Night Music Club

| • Album sales: 7,600,000 | • Release date: August 1993 |

Former backing vocalist, Sheryl Crow proved hard work for A&M when the singer-songwriter abandoned an entire debut-album's worth of material in favour of working with Bill Bottrell. The result, *Tuesday Night Music Club* reflected her rock roots, while propelling her to international stardom.

In the early 1990s Crow fell in with a Los Angeles-based collective who would meet every Tuesday to write songs, drink beer and exchange ideas. Consisting of several songwriters and producers, the group – which included David Ricketts, Brian McLeod, David Baerwald and Bill Bottrell – dubbed themselves the Tuesday Night Music Club. Inspired by the creative spirit of the group Crow collaborated with them to produce her new, improved debut.

*Tuesday Night Music Club* was slow to catch on. The first single, 'Run, Baby, Run' failed to chart, and sales of the second single, 'Leaving Las Vegas' (featured in the film of the same name), were weak. It was the third single, the infectious 'All I Wanna Do' that brought the album to the public's attention. Peaking at Number Two in the US, the song proved to be the biggest selling single of the summer of 1994. A fourth single, 'Strong Enough', became a Top Five hit. *Tuesday Night Music Club eventually* peaked at Number Three in the Billboard chart

| | |
|---|---|
| **Number One singles:** None | **Personnel:** Sheryl Crow Bill Bottrell David Baerwald Wendell Crow David Rickett, Dan Schwartz Kevin Gilbert Brian Macleod |
| **Grammy awards:** Record of the year; Best new artist; Best female pop vocal performance | |
| **Label:** US & UK: A&M | |
| **Recorded in:** Pasadena, USA | **Producer:** Bill Bottrell |

1  **Run, Baby, Run**  (4:53)
2  **Leaving Las Vegas**  (5:10)
3  **Strong Enough**  (3:10)
4  **Can't Cry Anymore**  (3:41)
5  **Solidify**  (4:08)
6  **The Na-Na Song**  (3:12)
7  **No One Said It Would Be Easy**  (5:29)
8  **What I Can Do For You**  (4:15)
9  **All I Wanna Do**  (4:32)
10  **We Do What We Can**  (5:38)
11  **I Shall Believe**  (5:34)

Total album length: 50 minutes

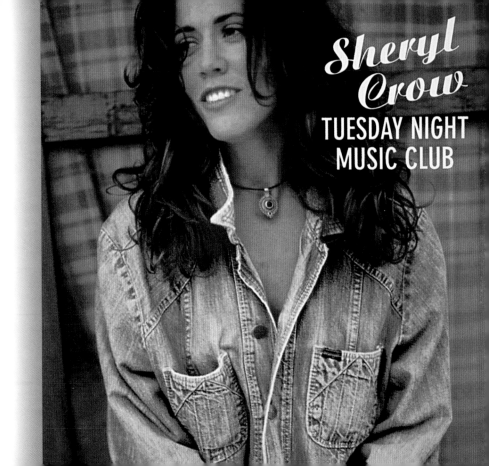

# 64 Savage Garden

| • **Album sales:** 7,600,000 | • **Release date:** April 1997 |

Following the release of their self-titled debut, Brisbane-based duo Savage Garden became the first Australian act to simultaneously top both the album and singles charts in its homeland. With their retro-brand of anthemic synth-pop, Savage Garden soon became an international success due, in part, to extensive airplay.

Compared to everyone from Roxette to Duran Duran, Savage Garden were not embraced by critics following the release of their debut album. However, the duo forged an increasingly large fanbase with a string of catchy singles, such as 'To the Moon and Back' and the US Number One 'Truly Madly Deeply'.

The month following the album's release, the act gained crucial exposure in the US when Rosie O'Donnell started playing parts of the track 'I Want You' on her talk show, before inviting them on to perform an acoustic version.

Consisting largely of melodic upbeat pop, *Savage Garden* showcased singer Darren Hayes' passionate vocal style while former Air Supply producer Charles Fisher's polished work ensured mainstream appeal. *Savage Garden* proved particularly popular in the US and UK, but nowhere more so than Australia, where it spent 19 weeks at the peak of the album chart.

**Number One singles:**
US: Truly Madly Deeply

**Grammy awards:** None

**Label:** US & UK: Columbia

**Recorded in:**
Brisbane, Australia

**Personnel:**
Darren Hayes
Daniel Jones
Rex Goh
Alex Hewitson
Terapai Richmond
Jacki Orzaczky

**Producers:**
Charles Fisher
Darren Hayes
Daniel Jones

1  To The Moon & Back (5:41)
2  I Want You (3:52)
3  Truly Madly Deeply (4:38)
4  Tears Of Pearls (3:47)
5  Universe (4:20)
6  Carry On Dancing (3:45)
7  Violet (4:04)
8  Break Me Shake Me (3:23)
9  A Thousand Words (4:00)
10 Promises (3:31)
11 Santa Monica (3:34)

Total album length: 42 minutes

# 63 No Need To Argue

| • **Album sales:** 7,900,000 | • **Release date:** October 1994 |

Following the success of their debut album *Everybody Else Is Doing It, So Why Can't We?*, the Cranberries stuck to the winning formula of lush epic pop for their career-defining second album *No Need To Argue*.

Recorded in the US and UK, *No Need to Argue* found the Irish quartet teaming up again with former Smiths' producer Stephen Street to build rousing orchestral soundscapes around the ethereal voice of Dolores O'Riordan. Much of the album's lyrical content is tied up in the troubles in Northern Ireland, not least 'Ode To My Family', an evocative song about the children of Belfast. The song opens with O'Riordan's subtle string arrangements, before she repeatedly passionately enquires 'Does anyone care?'

'Zombie', proved hugely popular on both sides of the Atlantic. It peaked at Number 14 in the UK and stayed on the singles chart for six weeks. Although it was never released as a single in the US, it became one of the most played songs on alternative radio. The other three UK singles, 'Ode To My Family', 'I Can't Be With You' and 'Ridiculous Thoughts' all made the Top 20.

*No Need To Argue* proved an instant success, selling 1,000,000 copies in its first three weeks of release. It peaking at Number Six on the Billboard Top 200 chart.

| **Number One singles:** | **Personnel:** |
|---|---|
| None | Dolores O'Riordan |
| | Noel Hogan |
| **Grammy awards:** None | Mike Hogan |
| | Feargal Lawler |

**Label:** US: Polygram
UK: Island

**Producer:**
Stephen Street

**Recorded in:** New York, USA; London & Oxford, UK

1  **Ode To My Family** (4:30)
2  **I Can't Be With You** (3:07)
3  **Twenty-One** (3:08)
4  **Zombie** (5:06)
5  **Empty** (3:26)
6  **Everything I Said** (3:53)
7  **The Icicle Melts** (2:54)
8  **Disappointment** (4:14)
9  **Ridiculous Thoughts** (4:31)
10 **Dreaming My Dreams** (3:37)
11 **Yeat's Grave** (2:59)
12 **Daffodil Lament** (6:09)
13 **No Need To Argue** (2:56)

Total album length: 50 minutes

the cranberries

no need to argue

# 62 (What's The Story) Morning Glory

| • Album sales: 7,900,000 | • Release date: October 1995 |

Released at the height of the UK Brit-Pop explosion *(What's The Story) Morning Glory* marked the first time Oasis made any real impact in the US, peaking at Number Four on the Billboard albums chart.

Fronted by former Inspiral Carpets roadie Noel Gallagher and his vocalist brother Liam, Oasis reached the peak of their fame with their sophomore album. Hailed in the UK as the new Beatles, Oasis became newspaper favourites due to their celebrity wives and public conflicts. The hype worked and as Liam Gallagher challenged George Harrison to a fight on London's Primrose Hill the album went multi-platinum.

Co-produced by Owen Morris and Noel Gallagher, and recorded at Rockfield Studios in Wales, *(What's The Story) Morning Glory* is a retrospective trawl through 1960s pop and psychedelia, borrowing heavily from the likes of the Small Faces and the Kinks.

Given the album's success in the US, sales of the singles were disappointing. 'Don't Look Back In Anger', a UK Number One, peaked at Number 55, while the other UK chart topper, 'Some Might Say', wasn't even released as a single.

The single 'Wonderwall' was nominated for a Grammy award for Best Rock Song and Best Rock Performance.

**Number One singles:**
UK: Don't Look Back In Anger; Some Might Say

**Grammy awards:** None

**Label:** US: Epic;
UK: Creation

**Recorded in:**
South Wales, UK

**Personnel:**
Noel Gallagher
Liam Gallagher
Paul Arthurs
Paul McGuigan
Alan White
Paul Weller
Tony McCarroll

**Producer:**
Owen Morrris
Noel Gallagher

1  Hello (3:32)
2  Roll With It (4:00)
3  Wonderwall (4:19)
4  Don't Look Back in Anger (4:48)
5  Hey Now! (5:41)
6  [untitled] (0:45)
7  Some Might Say (5:29)
8  Cast No Shadow (4:52)
9  She's Electric (3:41)
10 Morning Glory (5:03)
11 [untitled] (0:40)
12 Champagne Supernova (7:28)

Total album length: 50 minutes

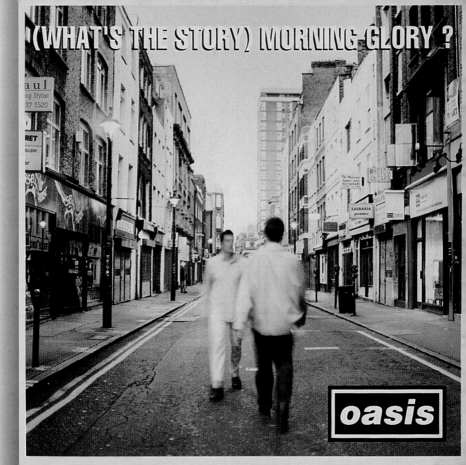

(WHAT'S THE STORY) MORNING GLORY ?

oasis

# 61 The Chase

| • Album sales: 8,000,000 | • Release date: October 1992 |

Recorded in Nashville and showcasing an increasingly open-minded and eclectic approach, *The Chase* showed little regard for the traditional boundaries of contemporary county music. Blending classic country and 1970s rock influences, Brooks paved the way for a whole generation of new country pretenders. *The Chase* contains tender moments, such as the cut 'Somewhere Other than the Night', as well as a feisty cover of Little Feat's 'Dixie Chicken' and the rousing 'Face to Face'.

The gospel-backed, anthemic album opener and first single 'We Shall Be Free' certainly sent shivers down the spine of many country DJs – the track fell short of radio playlists across the US, and the single peaked at a relatively disappointing Number 12 on the Billboard chart.

Despite the single's initial negative reception, the album took the Number One spot in the US and shifted more than five million copies before the year was out. Nonetheless *The Chase* sold only half as much as Brooks' previous two albums – enough to make a hit by anyone else's standards, but not enough to prevent media speculation that Brooks' career might be on a downward spiral.

**Number One singles:**
None

**Grammy awards:** None

**Label:** US & UK: Capitol

**Recorded in:**
Nashville, USA

**Personnel:**
Garth Brooks
Trisha Yearwood
Mark Casstevens
Chris Leuzinger
Bruce Bouton

Rob Hajacos
Denis Solee
Bobby Wood
Mike Chapman
Milton Sledge
Donna McElroy
Vicki Hampton
Yvonne Hodges
Debbie Nims
Gary Chapman
Howard Smith
Johnny Cobb

**Producers:**
John McBride
Allen Reynolds

1  We Shall Be Free  (3:48)
2  Somewhere Other Than The Night  (3:12)
3  Mr Right  (2:01)
4  Every Now And Then  (4:16)
5  Walking After Midnight  (2:33)
6  Dixie Chicken  (4:25)
7  Learning To Live Again  (4:06)
8  That Summer  (4:46)
9  Something With A Ring to It  (2:33)
10 Night Rider's Lament  (4:05)
11 Face To Face  (4:26)

Total album length: 37 minutes

**Garth Brooks**

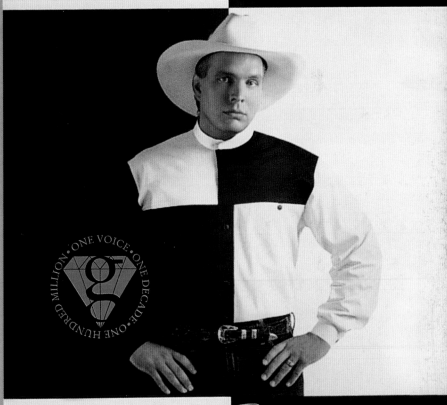

GARTH BROOKS

The Chase

ONE VOICE · ONE DECADE · ONE HUNDRED MILLION

# 60 Mi Tierra

| • **Album sales:** 8,000,000 | • **Release date:** June 1993 |

Cuban-American singer Gloria Estefan's first US Spanish-language album, *Mi Tierra*, is a truly international affair, having been recorded in no less than five studios in three countries on two continents. Masterfully reinterpreting traditional Afro-Cuban styles, *Mi Tierra* finds Estefan singing in Spanish, while a team of some of Latin music's most respected exponents, including the 79-year-old creator of mambo, Israel Lopez, offer support.

Overflowing with upbeat breezy tracks such as 'Montuno' and 'Hablemos el Mismo Idioma', and melodious ballads, such as 'Con Los Anos Que Me Quedan', *Mi Tierra* exposed Estefan as far more that just another pop princess. Working alongside arranger Juanito Marquez, and singer and percussionist Luis Enrique, Estefan reclaimed her roots in exquisite style.

*Mi Tierra* was received warmly by critics across the board, and is widely regarded as one of Estefan's finest albums. Although one might think it is her least commercial album, it is in fact her biggest-selling album to date and peaked at Number 27 in the US, spawning the hit singles 'Tradicion' and 'Con Los Anos Que Me Quedan'. *Mi Tierra* won the singer a Grammy for Best Tropical Latin Album in 1993.

**Number One singles:**
None

**Grammy awards:** Best tropical Latin album

**Label:** US & UK: Epic

**Recorded in:** London & Hampstead, UK; Miami, USA; Madrid, Spain

**Producers:**
Jorge Casas
Clay Ostwald
Emilio Estefan Jr

**Personnel:**
Gloria Estefan
Juanito R Marquez
Nestor Torres
Paquito D'Rivera
Mannie Lopez
Teddy Mulet
Cheito Quinonez
Randy Barlow
Paquito Hechavarria
Israel Lopez
Luis Enrique
Sheila E
Tito Puente

1 Con Los Años Que Me Quedan (4:37)
2 Mi Tierra (4:38)
3 Ayer (5:17)
4 Mi Buen Amor (3:50)
5 Tus Ojos (4:11)
6 No Hay Mal Que Por Bien No V (5:28)
7 Sí Señor, Es Mi Son (4:40)
8 Volverás (3:55)
9 Montuno (4:57)
10 Hablemos el Mismo Idioma (4:45)
11 Hablas De Mí (3:40)
12 Tradición (5:21)

Total album length: 52 minutes

**Gloria Estefan**

# 59 Miracles: The Holiday Album

| • **Album sales:** 8,000,000 | • **Release date:** September 1994 |

Largely produced and arranged by Kenny G and long-time associate Walter Afanasieff, Kenny G's *Miracles: The Holiday Album* proved a hugely popular Christmas hit. The album contained an array of jazz standards, carols and traditional seasonal pieces. Recorded at Studio G & Ocean Way Studios and released four months before Christmas, the album peaked at Number One on the Billboard chart.

Regarded by fans as 'the' holiday jazz album, *Miracles* was inspired in part by the birth of Kenny G's son. The album is packed with easy-listening melodic jazz. A seasonal romantic feel is maintained throughout with tracks such as 'Winter Wonderland,' 'Silent Night' and 'White Christmas' setting the tone while Kenny G's soprano saxophone provides the centrepoint. Among the reworking of timeless seasonal classics on the Seattle-born instrumentalist's album, 'Have Yourself A Merry Little Christmas' proved particularly popular, and was nominated for a Grammy for Best Pop Instrumental Performance.

Kenny G and his soprano horn also take on the self-penned 'The Chanukah Song', and even performed Brahms' 'Lullaby'. The most amusing moment during the album's relatively short 35-minute running time has to be a reading of 'Greensleeves' bound to Dave Brubeck's 'Take 5'.

| **Number One singles:** | **Personnel:** |
|---|---|
| None | Kenny G |
| | Dann Huff |
| **Grammy awards:** None | Walter Afanasieff |
| | Randy Jackson |
| **Label:** US: Arista UK: BMG | John Robinson |
| **Recorded in:** | **Producers:** |
| California, USA | Kenny G |
| | Walter Afanasieff |

1  **Winter Wonderland**  (3:00)
2  **White Christmas**  (2:59)
3  **Have Yourself A Merry Little Christmas**  (3:54)
4  **Silent Night**  (3:44)
5  **Greensleeves**  (3:26)
6  **Miracles**  (2:30)
7  **The Little Drummer Boy**  (4:02)
8  **The Chanukah Song**  (2:28)
9  **Silver Bells**  (3:57)
10 **Away in A Manger**  (2:36)
11 **Brahms' Lullaby**  (3:13)

Total album length: 35 minutes

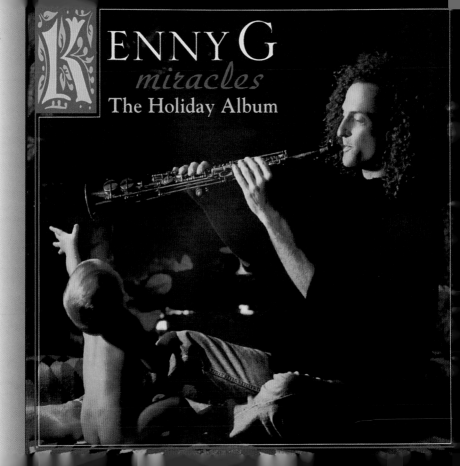

# KENNY G
## *miracles*
### The Holiday Album

# 58 Surfacing

| • Album sales: 8,000,000 | • Release date: July 1997 |

Released to coincide with the start of the first Lillith Fair tour, *Surfacing* was a hugely successful showcase for Vancouver-based singer-songwriter Sarah McLachlan. As the event's organizer, McLachlan found herself on the cover of magazines across the US. It was in this flurry of media hype that *Surfacing*, her fifth album, debuted at Number Two on the US charts, 48 places higher than her previous album.

Working alongside long-time producer and collaborator, Daniel Lanois' protégée Pierre Marchand, McLachlan presented her most mature work yet. With her soaring, remarkably versatile voice exploring the darker side of humanity *Surfacing* is an introspective, evocative work of gentle beauty. Among the pastoral, melodic songs 'Sweet Surrender', the ballad 'I Love You', and the heart wrenching 'Angel' are among the most effective. 'Angel' found its way to Number Four on the Billboard Hot 100 single chart, while 'Adia' hit Number Three.

McLachlan won two Grammy awards in 1997, Best Female Pop Vocal Performance for the single 'Building A Mystery' and Best Pop Instrumental Performance with 'Last Dance'.

**Number One singles:**
None

**Grammy awards:**
Best Female Pop Vocal
Performance – Building A
Maystery; Best Pop
Instrumental Performance
– Last Dance

**Label:** US & UK: Arista

**Recorded in:**
Quebec, Canada

**Personnel:**
Sarah McLachlan
Brian Minato
Michel Pepin
Yves Desrosiers
Ash Sood
Pierre Marchand
Jim Creeggan

**Producer:**
Pierre Marchand

1  **Building A Mystery** (4:07)
2  **I Love You** (4:44)
3  **Sweet Surrender** (4:00)
4  **Adia** (4:05)
5  **Do What You Have To Do** (3:47)
6  **Witness** (4:45)
7  **Angel** (4:30)
8  **Black And White** (5:02)
9  **Full Of Grace** (3:41)
10 **Last Dance** (2:33)

Total album length: 41 minutes

# 57 Breathe

| • Album sales: 8,000,000 | • Release date: November 1999 |

Having tested the water with her third album, *Faith*, country superstar Faith Hill dived straight in to the pop mainstream with *Breathe*, now singing about making not losing it. In fact five of the album's 13 songs have love in the title, and virtually all concentrate on the subject, from the jubilant 'I Got My Baby', and the heart-warming harmonies of 'The Way You Love Me', to the soulful 'Love is A Sweet Thing'. The change in lyrical tone no doubt owes much to her marriage to country heartthrob Tim McGraw, and the recent birth of her second child.

Breathe is a smooth blend of rock, pop, R&B and gospel with just a sprinkling of country to add favour with the fanbase. The album went straight into the Billboard 200 chart at Number One and won three Grammy awards the following year. Not only did the album garner the award for Best Country Album and Best Female Country Vocal Performance, but the duet with her husband on 'Let's Make Love' won Best Country Collaboration With Vocals.

**Number One singles:**
None

**Grammy awards:**
Best country album; Best female country vocal performance; Best country collaboration with vocals – Let's Make Love

**Label:** US: Warner; UK: 404 Music

**Recorded in:**
Nashville, USA

**Personnel:**
Faith Hill
Tim McGraw
B James Lowry
Larry Byrom
Dann Huff
Gordon Kennedy
John Willis
Michael Landau
Paul Franklin
Gary Smith
Aubrey Haynie
Various other personnel

**Producers:**
Faith Hill
Byron Gallimore
Dann Huff

1 What's In It For Me (5:36)
2 I Got My Baby (3:31)
3 Love Is A Sweet Thing (3:56)
4 Breathe (4:09)
5 Let's Make Love (4:11)
6 It Will Be Me (3:46)
7 The Way You Love Me (3:06)
8 If I'm Not In Love (4:02)
9 Bringing Out Elvis (3:34)
10 If My Heart Had Wings (3:35)
11 If I Should Fall Behind (4:32)
12 That's How Love Moves (4:14)
13 There Will Come A Day (4:15)

Total album length: 52 minutes

FAITH HILL
BREATHE

# 56 Core

• **Album sales:** 8,100,000 | • **Release date:** September 1992 |

At the height of early-1990s grunge explosion, while all eyes were on Seattle, the Stone Temple Pilots put San Diego's music scene on the map with *Core*, their debut album. Heaving with emotive rock echoing the work of Led Zeppelin, the roots of the band owe more to the arena rock of the 1970s than the Sex Pistols or Neil Young. Indeed, the origins of the band can be traced back to Mighty Joe Young, a Californian heavy metal band.

Scott Weiland's thunderous baritone voice carries powerful messages throughout the album, not least on tracks such as 'Dead And Bloated', a tirade against apathy, and 'Sex Type Thing', on which he takes on the subject of rape and which he would often play live wearing a dress to add emphasis. However, it was Dean DeLeo's memorable guitar hook, heaving behind Weiland's anthemic vocal, that provided the power behind hit single 'Plush', a song that finally elevated the band above the status of mere grunge imitators.

*Core* proved to be a slow burner when it came to sales, not making the US Top 20 until the summer of 1993, on the back of a heavy year of touring. *Core* eventually peaked at Number Three, paving the way for their chart-topping follow-up, *Purple*, in 1994. That same year, Stone Temple Pilots won a Grammy award for Best Hard Rock Performance With Vocal for 'Plush'.

**Number One singles:**
None

**Grammy awards:** Best hard rock performance with vocal

**Label:** US & UK: Atlantic

**Recorded in:**
Los Angeles, USA

**Personnel:**
Dean DeLeo
Robert DeLeo
Eric Kretz
Scott Weiland

**Producer:**
Brenden O'Brien

1 Dead And Bloated (5:11)
2 Sex Type Thing (3:38)
3 Wicked Garden (4:05)
4 No Memory (1:20)
5 Sin (6:04)
6 Naked Sunday (3:49)
7 Creep (5:32)
8 Piece Of Pie (5:24)
9 Plush (5:13)
10 Wet My Bed (1:37)
11 Crackerman (3:14)
12 Where The River Goes (8:26)

Total Album length: 53 minutes

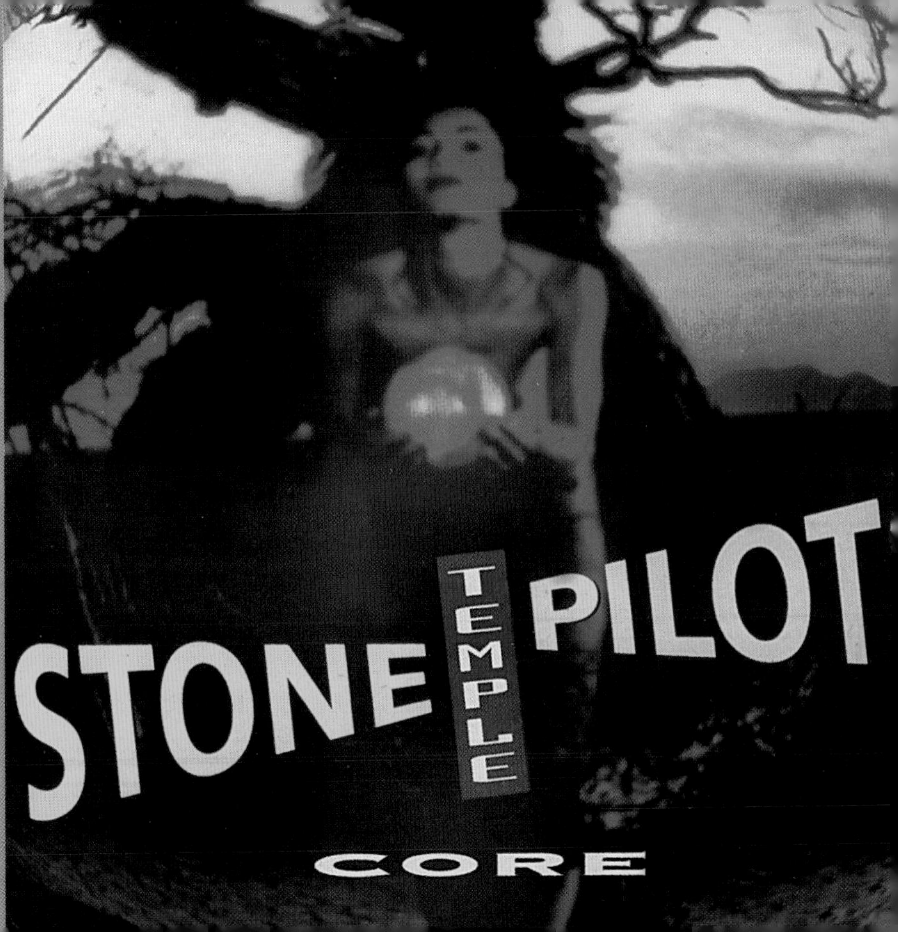
STONE TEMPLE PILOT
CORE

## 55 Toni Braxton

| • Album sales: 8,100,000 | • Release date: July 1993 |

Toni Braxton was the first female artist to sign to LaFace – the label set up by producers Babyface and LA Reid – and her solo debut album was highly anticipated.

**Number One singles:**
None

**Grammys:** Best new artist – Another Sad Love Song; Best female R&B vocal performance (1993 & 1994) – Breathe Again

**Label:** US: LaFace; UK: Arista

**Recorded in:**
Atlanta, USA

**Personnel:**
Toni Braxton
Vassal Benford
Vincent Herbert
Ben Garrison
Noelle Groin
McArthur
Tomi M
Ernesto Phillips
Skip Pruitt

Vance Taylor
Tim Thomas
Ted Bishop
Bo Watson
Rex Rideout
Kayo
Orlando Phillips
L A Reid
DeRock
Pamela Copeland
Tammy Davis
Keisha Jackson
Ty-V
Trina Broussard
Valerie Davis

**Producers:**
LA Reid
Babyface
Ted
Tim
Toni Braxton
Bo
Vincent Herbert
Various other producers

Groomed by the duo as the 'first lady of LaFace', *Toni Braxton* certainly didn't disappoint, going on to earn the sultry-voiced R&B singer three Grammy awards, including the 1993 Best New Artist Award. With the songwriting and production team keeping the mood diverse, Braxton was given room to exercise her husky, soulful voice in a myriad of emotive settings with 'Another Sad Love Song' and 'Seven Whole Days' proving the perfect vehicles to showcase her vocal gymnastics.

*Toni Braxton* climbed to the pinnacle of the Billboard 200 and spawned a string of Top 10 singles, including 'Another Sad Love Song', 'Breathe Again' and 'You Mean The World To Me'.

1 Another Sad Love Song  (5:01)
2 Breathe Again  (4:29)
3 Seven Whole Days  (6:22)
4 Love Affair  (4:28)
5 Candlelight  (4:36)
6 Spending My Time With You  (4:08)
7 Love Shoulda Brought You Home  (4:56)
8 I Belong To You  (3:53)
9 How Many Ways  (4:45)
10 You Mean The World To Me  (4:53)
11 Best Friend  (4:28)
12 Breathe Again  (Reprise)  (1:19)

Total album length: 53 minutes

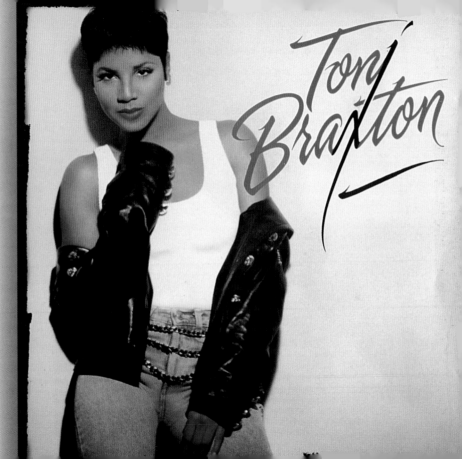

Toni Braxton

# **54** In Pieces

| • Album sales: 8,100,000 | • Release date: August 1993 |

Recorded at Jack's Track's Recording Studio, Nashville, Tennessee, Garth Brooks' sixth album, *In Pieces*, found the star at the height of his popularity, edging away form traditional country in favour of upbeat rock-influenced tracks and dramatic ballads.

On *In Pieces* Brooks embraced the high drama and low pace of country pop, influenced greatly by Billy Joel. Demonstrating an inimitable cross-over style that would ultimately see him shift over 100 million albums in the US alone, the album finds Brooks flirting with Cajun on 'Callin' Baton Rouge', before finally returning to his roots for the closing track 'The Cowboy Song'.

While shying away from the overt eclecticism of Brooks' previous two albums, *In Pieces* generated five hits singles, including 'Ain't Going Down (Til The Sun Comes Up)' and 'American Honkey-Tonk Bar Association'. The album became Brooks' third to enter the Billboard charts at Number One. That same year saw Brooks perform the 'Star Spangled Banner' to an estimated TV audience of a billion people in 87 countries during pre-game festivities at the Super Bowl.

**Number One singles:**
None

**Grammy awards:** None

**Label: US & UK:** Capitol

**Recorded In:**
Nashville, USA

**Personnel:**
Garth Brooks
Chris Leuzinger
Ty England
Mark Casstevens
Steve McClure
Bruce Bouton
Jerry Douglas
Rob Hajacos
Terry McMillan
Jim Horn
Bobby Wood
Bobby Emmons
Mike Chapman
Roy Huskey Jr
Milton Sledge
Mike Palmer
Ferrell Morris
Helen Darling
Kathy Chiavola
Trisha Yearwood

**Producer:**
Allen Reynolds

1  **Standing Outside The Fire** (3:52)
2  **The Night I Called The Old Man Out** (3:12)
3  **American Honkey-Tonk Bar Association** (3:33)
4  **One Night A Day** (4:15)
5  **Ain't Going Down (Til The Sun Comes Up)** (4:33)
6  **Anonymous** (2:56)
7  **Kickin' And Screamin'** (4:02)
8  **The Red Strokes** (3:44)
9  **Callin' Baton Rouge** (2:38)
10 **The Night Will Only Know** (3:55)
11 **The Cowboy Song** (3:59)

Total album length: 37 minutes

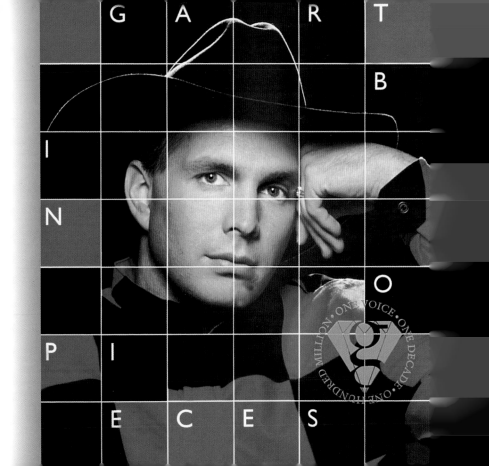

# 53 Throwing Copper

| • Album sales: 8,100,000 | • Release date: April 1994 |

With former Talking Heads guitarist Jerry Harrison behind the production desk and Edward Kolaczyk's aching, emotional lyrics, *Throwing Copper* proved to be Live's most successful album and contained some of the Philadelphia quartet's most cohesive work.

Clearly influenced by grunge and the intensity of acts such as Nirvana and REM, *Throwing Copper* opens with the sinister murderous tale 'The Dam at Otter Creek', before taking on a wealth of provocative subject matter. 'White Discussion' finds Kolaczyk extolling a bilious, rage-fuelled vision of an apocalyptic dying earth.

The album spawned three hit singles, 'Selling The Drama', 'I Alone' and 'Lightning Crashes', the latter written in remembrance of Barbara Lewis, a classmate of Kolaczyk's who was killed by a drunk driver in 1993.

The released of *Throwing Copper* prompted the band to undertake an 18-month, 252-show world tour that included Woodstock, while somehow finding time to appear on *Saturday Night Live* and *MTV Unplugged*. The strenuous promotional schedule paid off with the band being voted Rock Artist of the Year at the 1995 Billboard Music Awards. The album made its way to the peak of the charts in the US, a feat the band repeated three years later with their follow-up album *Secret Samadhi*. In the UK it peaked at Number 37.

**Number One singles:**
None

**Grammy awards:** None

**Label:** US & UK:
Radioactive

**Recorded in:**
Cannon Falls, USA

**Personnel:**
Edward Kowalczyk
Chad Taylor
Patrick Dahlheimer
Chad Gracey

**Producer:**
Jerry Harrison
Edward Kowalczyk
Chad Taylor
Patrick Dahlheimer
Chad Gracey

| | |
|---|---|
| 1 Dam At Otter Creek (4:43) | 9 T B D (4:28) |
| 2 Selling The Drama (3:20) | 10 Stage (3:08) |
| 3 I Alone (3:50) | 11 Waitress (2:49) |
| 4 Iris (3:59) | 12 Pillar Of Davidson (6:46) |
| 5 Lightning Crashes (5:25) | 13 White, Discussion (6:08) |
| 6 Top (2:42) | 14 [untitled] (4:16) |
| 7 All Over You (3:59) | |
| 8 Shit Towne (3:48) | Total album length: 52 minutes |

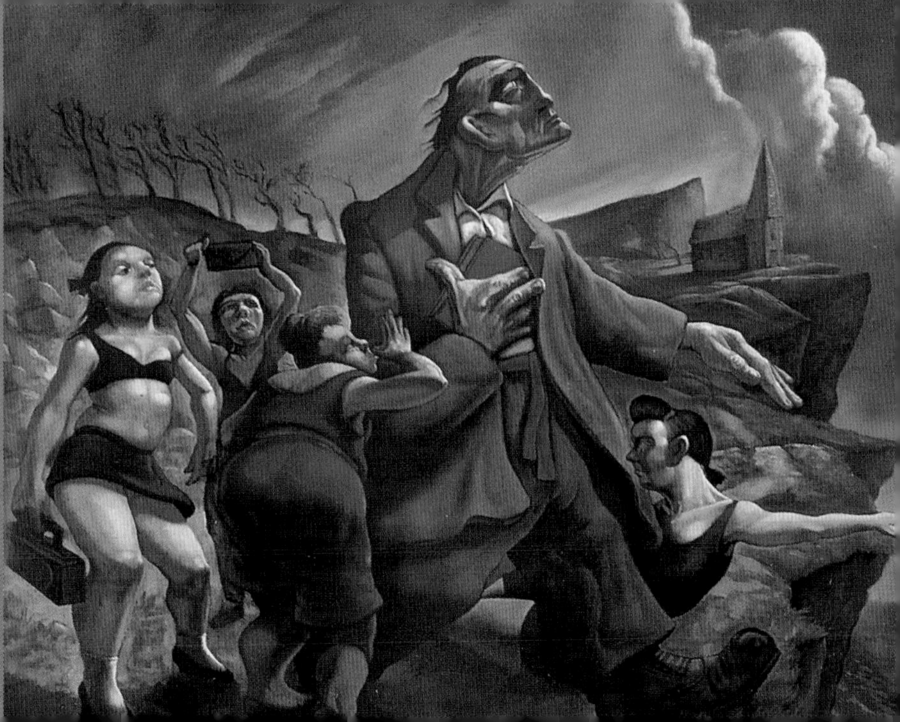

Sleeve artwork by Tim Stedman

# 52 All Eyez On Me

| • Album sales: 8,100,000 | • Release date: February 1996 |

The first double album of original material in hip-hop history and certainly one of the most nihilistic releases to take residence atop the *Billboard* 200 album chart, Tupac Shakur's *All Eyez On Me* mixes venomous rap with slickly produced good-time beats.

A blistering beat-driven lyrical tirade at life's injustices, *All Eyez On Me* finds Shakur being joined at the microphone by a wealth of talent including rappers Snoop Dogg and Dr Dre and godfather of funk George Clinton. The album was nominated for a Grammy for Best Rap Album, while the singles 'California Love', featuring Dr. Dre and Roger Troutman, and 'How Do U Want It', featuring KC and JoJo, were also nominated.

Just seven months after the album's release Shakur was killed in a drive-by shooting.

**Number One singles:**
US: How Do U Want It

**Grammy awards:** None

**Label:**
US & UK: Death Row

**Recorded In:**
Tarzana, USA

**Producers:**
Dr Dre
David Blake
Bobby Ervi
DJ Pooh
Doug Rasheed
Micheal Mosley
Various other producers

**Personnel:**
Tupac Shakur (d. 1996)
George Clinton
Richie Rich
Dr Dre
Yani Hadati
Redman
Jojo the Elf
Snoop Dogg
Rappin' 4-Tay
Jewell
Big Syke
Roger Troutman
Danny Ray
Michel'le
Various other personnel

1  Ambitionz Az A Ridah (4:39)
2  All Bout U (4:37)
3  Skandalouz (4:09))
4  Got My Mind Made Up (5:13)
5  How Do U Want It (4:47)
6  2 Of Amerikaz Most Wanted (4:07)
7  No More Pain (6:14)
8  Heartz Of Men (4:43)
9  Life Goes On (5:02)
10  Only God Can Judge Me (4:57)
11  Tradin War Stories (5:29)
12  California Love (6:25)
13  I Ain't Mad At Cha (4:53)
14  What'z Ya Phone # (5:10)
15  Can't C Me (5:30)
16  Shorty Wanna Be A Thug (3:51)
17  Holla At Me (4:56)
18  Wonda Why They Call U Bytch (4:19)
19  When We Ride (5:09)
20  Thug Passion (5:08)
21  Picture Me Rollin' (5:15)
22  Check Out Time (4:39)
23  Ratha Be Ya Nigga (4:14)
24  All Eyez On Me (5:08)
25  Run tha Streetz (5:17)
26  Ain't Hard 2 Find (4:29)
27  Heaven Ain't Hard 2 Find (3:58)

Total album length: 132 minutes

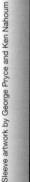

# 2PAC

### all eyez on me

**2** COMPACT DISC FIRST EDITION

DIGITALLY REMASTERED

# 51 Christina Aguilera

| • **Album sales:** 8,100,000 | • **Release date:** August 1999 |

Following in the footsteps of Britney Spears and two members of *N Sync, Christina Aguilera became the next alumni of the Disney's *New Mickey Mouse Club* to hit the charts.

Released when the singer was aged only 18, *Christina Aguilera* followed the success of the first single 'Genie In A Bottle', a polished dose of pop that had topped the US charts for five weeks. Written by UK-based songwriter Pam Sheyne, the track became the biggest-selling US single of the year and was also a Number One hit in the UK. The album debuted at Number One on the US chart, outselling Puff Daddy's *Forever* by almost 50,000 copies. Propelled to stardom, the new princess of teen-pop soon found herself performing at the White House Christmas gala and featuring in the Super Bowl halftime show.

**Number One singles:**
US & UK: Genie In A Bottle
US: What A Girl Wants;
Come On Over Baby (All I
Want is You)

**Grammy awards:**
Best new artist

**Label:** US & UK: RCA

**Recorded In:** N/A

**Personnel:**
Christina Aguilera
Steve Kipner
Michael Thompson
Evan Rogers
Sue Ann Carwell
Ron Fair
John Goux
Shelly Peiken
Tim Pierce
Travon Potts
Carl Sturken

Matt Laug
Dave Frank
Ali Boudris
Heather Holley
Paul Rein
John Glaser
Bruce Watson
Anthony Mazza

**Producers:**
Mathew Wilder
Steve Kipner
Evan Rogers
Ron Harris
Travon Potts
Guy Roche
Carl Sturken
Diane Warren
Aaron Zigman
Robin Thicke
Dave Frank
Sturkin
Rogers
Doreem Dorian
Johan Aberg

1  Genie In A Bottle  (3:36)
2  What A Girl Wants  (3:52)
3  I Turn To You  (4:33)
4  So Emotional  (4:00)
5  Come On Over (All I Want Is You)  (3:09)
6  Reflection  (3:33)
7  Love For All Seasons  (3:59)
8  Somebody's Somebody  (5:03)
9  When You Put Your Hands On Me  (3:35)
10 Blessed  (3:05)
11 Love Will Find A Way  (3:56)
12 Obvious  (4:00)

Total album length: 46 minutes

**christina aguilera**

# 50 R.

| • **Album sales:** 8,300,000 | • **Release date:** November 1998 |

R. Kelly was already considered a talented and prolific composer, singer and producer before the release of *R*, but few expected the star to deliver over two hours of music with his fourth solo album. It followed the massive success of his 1997 US Number Two single

'I Believe I Can Fly' (recorded for the film *Space Jam*, but also appearing here), which had won Kelly three Grammy awards.

Among the other hits featured is 'I'm Your Angel', a duet with Celine Dion, which earned Kelly the second US Number One single of his career. Other guest stars include Keith Murray on the laid-back, funky opener 'Home Alone' and some of rap's hottest talents including Cam'Ron and Norega, Jay Z and Nas.

**Number One singles:**
US: I'm Your Angel;
UK: I Believe I Can Fly

**Grammy awards:**
Best male R&B vocal
performance – I Believe
I Can Fly; Best R&B song
– I Believe I Can Fly; Best
song written for a motion
picture or television –
I Blieve I Can Fly

**Label:** US & UK: Jive

**Recorded in:**
Various locations, USA

**Personnel:**
R. Kelly
Tone
Rob Bacon

Cam'Ron
Norega
Jeff Vereb
G-One
LaFayette Carthon Jr
Blake Chaffin
Anthony Kilhoffer
Joey Donnatello
Kelly Price
Nas
Rock
Celine Dion
Foxy Brown
Jay-Z
Various other personnel

**Producers:**
R Kelly
G-One
Sean 'Puffy' Combs
Ron 'Amen-Ra' Lawrence
Various other producers

1 Home Alone (4:59)
2 Spendin' Money (4:54)
3 If I'm Wit You (4:31)
4 Half On A Baby (4:55)
5 When A Woman's Fed Up (4:38)
6 Get up On A Room (4:10)
7 One Man (4:57)
8 We Ride (4:49)
9 The Opera (1:25)
10 The Interview (1:33)
11 Only The Loot Can Make Me Happy (4:56)
12 Don't Put Me Out (5:22)
13 Suicide (5:19)
14 Etcetera (4:13)
15 If I Could Turn Back The Hands Of Time (6:18)

16 What I Feel/Issues (4:44)
17 The Chase (2:46)
18 V.I.P (4:16)
19 Did You Ever Think (4:32)
20 Dollar Bill (4:23)
21 Reality (4:44)
22 2nd Kelly (5:02)
23 Ghetto Queen (4:20)
24 Down Low Double Life (5:00)
25 Looking For Love (4:36)
26 Dancing With A Rich Man (3:28)
27 I'm Your Angel (5:20)
28 Money Makes The World Go Round (4:09)
29 I Believe I Can Fly (5:21)

Total album length: 129 minutes

R.

# 49 Secrets

| • **Album sales:** 8,600,000 | • **Release date:** June 1996 |

Toni Braxton combined sound, looks, voice and attitude to make her one of the decade's biggest R&B stars. *Secrets* was her second album, the follow-up to an eight-times-platinum eponymous debut, and it solidifies the formula that made that album so popular. *Secrets* is once again overseen by LA Reid and Babyface, on whose record label the album was released, with the help of some the day's hottest songwriters.

'Un-Break My Heart' was the album's defining song – this ballad was a good showcase for Braxton's deep, soulful voice, and David Foster's melody made the song one of 1995's biggest singles, securing it a Number One slot on the Billboard singles chart. The slinky, funky 'You're Makin' Me High' was teamed with the slower 'Let It Flow' (which originally appeared on the soundtrack to *Waiting To Exhale*) gave Braxton another Top 30 single. The album secured Braxton two Grammy awards in 1997.

**Number one singles:**
US: Un-Break My Heart

**Grammy awards:**
Best female pop vocal performance – Unbreak My Heart; Best female R&B vocal performance – You're Makin' Me High

**Label:** US: La Face;
UK: Arista

**Recorded in:**
Atlanta, Los Angeles & New York, USA

**Personnel:**
Toni Braxton
Tony Rich
R Kelly
Keith Crouch
Jeremy Lubbock
Dean Parks
Michael Thompson
Reggie Griffin
Kenny G
Greg Phillinganes
Kenneth Crouch
Reggie Hamilton
Nathan East
Luis Conte
Randy Walker
Andrea Martin
Various other personnel

**Producers:**
Tony Rich
LA Reid
Babyface
Bryce Wilson
David Foster

1  Come On Over Here  (3:36)
2  You're Makin' Me High  (4:26)
3  There's No Me Without You  (4:19)
4  Un-Break My Heart  (4:30)
5  Talking In His Sleep  (5:33)
6  How Could An Angel Break My Heart  (4:20)
7  Find Me A Man  (4:27)
8  Let It Flow  (4:21)
9  Why Should I Care  (4:25)
10 I Don't Want To  (4:170
11 I Love Me Some Him  (5:09)
12 In the Late Of Night/Toni's Secrets  (5:33)

Total album length: 55 minutes

Toni Braxton

Secrets

# 48 The Miseducation Of Lauryn Hill

| • **Album sales:** 8,600,000 | • **Release date:** August 1998 |

Of all the female singing stars of the decade, few made an album as distinctive and successful in its genre-splicing as Lauryn Hill. For her debut, the 23-year-old took her lead from the soul/hip-hop sound of former band the Fugees, broadening and deepening it to produce an album that was commercial and wildly popular.

The first single, 'Doo Wop (That Thing)' demonstrated the mix of styles that the album had to offer – rapped verses, Motown-powered horn section, a joyous chorus and cutting lyrics about sexuality infidelity. The result was a huge US Number One smash that reached Number Three in the UK.

Supporting the album are Carlos Santana's guitar on 'To Zion', Mary J. Blige on the haunting 'I Used To Love Him', and D'Angelo on the smooth 'Nothing Even Matters'.

**Number One singles:**
US: Doo Wop (That Thing)

**Grammys:** Album of the year; Best new artist; Best female R&B vocal performance – Doo Wop (That Thing); Best R&B song – Doo Wop (That Thing); Best R&B album

**Label:** US: Ruffhouse
UK: Columbia

**Recorded in:** New York & Miami, USA; London, UK; Kingston, Jamaica

**Personnel:**
Lauryn Hill
Mary J Blige
D'Angelo
Carlos Santana
Johari Newton
Robert Browne
Earl Chinna-Smith
Grace Paradise
Dean Frasier
Everol Ray
Nambo Robinson
Tejumold Newton
John R Stephens
Joe Wilson
James Poyser
Chris Meredith
Che Guevara
Tom Barney
Matthew Rubano
Paul Fakhourie
Jared Crawford
Ruby Byrd
Earl Robinson
Andrea Simmons
Kenny Bobien
Various other personnel

**Producers:**
Lauryn Hill
Vada Nobles
Che Guevara

1 Intro (0.47)
2 Lost Ones (5:33)
3 Ex-Factor (5:26)
4 To Zion (6:09)
5 Doo Wop (That Thing) (5:20)
6 Superstar (4:57)
7 Final Hour (4:16)
8 When It Hurts So Bad (5:42)
9 I Used To Love Him (5:39)
10 Forgive Them Father (5:15)
11 Every Ghetto, Every City (5:14)
12 Nothing Even Matters (5:50)
13 Everything Is Everything (4:53)
14 The Miseducation Of Lauryn Hill (4:17)
15 Can't Take My Eyes Off Of You (3:41)
16 Sweetest Thing (4:40)

Total album length: 78 minutes

# 47 Dangerous

| • **Album sales:** 8,800,000 | • **Release date:** November 1991 |

Despite the massive success of Michael Jackson's previous album Bad, there was the feeling that he had simply repeated the Thriller formula. Dangerous saw Jackson switch from Quincy Jones as producer to new-jack-swing king Terry Riley, who, in collaboration with Bruce Swedien and Bill Bottrell, infused the album with a harder, more contemporary dance sound.

The opening tracks jerk along on booming, reverb-heavy drums, stuttering bass, clipped funk guitars and Jackson's trademark yelping vocals. There's plenty of pop too though – the first single, 'Black Or White', features a guitar riff from Guns N' Roses' Slash.

*Dangerous* is a long album and many of the tracks cross the five minute mark. The sprawling video for 'Black Or White', which premiered simultaneously on MTV, VH1, BET and ABS, was over 10 minutes long. Despite this, the album spawned six singles, three of which – 'Black Or White', 'In The Closet' and 'Remember The Time' – placed in the US Top Ten. *Dangerous* also topped the albums charts on both sides of the Atlantic, making Jackson the first solo artist since Elton John in 1975 to hit the US Number One with three back-to-back releases.

**Number One singles:**
US & UK: Black Or White

**Grammy awards:** none

**Label:** US & UK: Epic

**Recorded in:**
Los Angeles, USA

**Personnel:**
Michael Jackson
Heavy D
Christa Larson
Teddy Riley
Paul Jackson Jr
Tim Pierce
David Williams
Slash
Larry Corbett

Jai Winding
David Paich
Steve Porcaro
Rene Moore
Greg Phillinganes
Bryan Loren
Abraham Laboriel
Jeff Porcaro
Wayne Cobham
Paulinho Da Costa
Siedah Garrett
Shanice Wilson
Various other personnel

**Producers:**
Michael Jackson
Teddy Riley
Bruce Swedien
Bill Bottrell

1  Jam  (5:39)
2  Why You Wanna Trip on Me  (5:24)
3  In The Closet  (6:32)
4  She Drives Me Wild  (3:42)
5  Remember The Time  (4:00)
6  Can't Let Her Get Away  (5:01)
7  Heal The World  (6:25)
8  Black Or White  (4:16)
9  Who Is It  (6:35)
10  Give In To Me  (5:29)
11  Will You Be There  (7:41)
12  Keep The Faith  (5:57)
13  Gone Too Soon  (3:22)
14  Dangerous  (7:00)

Total album length: 77 minutes

**Michael Jackson**

| • Album sales: 8,900,000 | • Release date: July 1999 |

Their second album, *The Writing's On The Wall* helped Destiny's Child cement their status as the world's number one R&B girl group, combining state-of-the-art and often inventive production with slick pop melodies and the group's distinctive vocals. The album's crack team of producers included Rodney Jerkins, Dwayne Wiggins and Missy Elliott, and although every track features a multitude of writing credits, the girls' personalities and attitude come through far stronger than on many similar albums. *The Writing's On The Wall* was also the last record to feature the four-piece version of Destiny's Child, although there was now little doubt that Beyoncé Knowles was the group's leader.

'Jumpin Jumpin', 'Bills, Bills, Bills' and 'Say My Name' were massive singles, the latter two hitting Number One in the US and Number Three in the UK. 'Say My Name' received two Grammy nominations. The group's stuttering rhythms and funky, cut-up instrumentions was a genuinely original sound that has been much imitated, while the lyrics, stressing the girl's independent status, formed a dedicated female fanbase.

**Number one singles:**
US: Say My Name; Bills Bills Bills

**Grammys:** Best R&B performance by a duo or group with vocal

**Label:** US & UK: Columbia

**Recorded in:** N/A

**Personnel:**
Kelly
La Tavia
Le Toya
Beyonce
Missy Elliot
Next
Byron Rittenhouse

Gerald Thomas
Donald Holmes
Anthony Hardy
Dwayne Wiggins
Charles Spikes
Sonny Lallerstedt
Vincent Lars
Bill Ortiz
Terry-T
Daryl Simmons
Ronnie Garrett
Raymond McKinnley
Various other personnel

**Producers:**
Kevin Briggs
Rodney Jerkins
Dwayne Wiggins
Chad Elliot
Missy Elliot

1 Intro (The Writing's On the Wall) (2:07)
2 So Good (3:14)
3 Bills, Bills, Bills (4:16)
4 Confessions (4:58)
5 Bug A Boo (3:31)
6 Temptation (4:06)
7 Now That She's Gone (5:35)
8 Where'd You Go (4:15)
9 Hey Ladies (4:16)
10 If You Leave (4:35)
11 Jumpin' Jumpin' (3:50)
12 Say My Name (4:31)
13 She Can't Love You (4:05)
14 Stay (4:51)
15 Sweet Sixteen (4:13)
16 Outro (2:39)

Total album length: 65 minutes

destiny's child | the writing's on the wall

Sleeve artwork by Albert Sanchez

# 45 Cooleyhighharmony

| • **Album sales:** 9,100,000 | • **Release date:** May 1991 |

One the most successful R&B acts of the decade, Boyz II Men combined classic four-piece close harmonies with a modern urban sound. *Cooleyhighharmony* was their debut album, and became the biggest-selling R&B album to that point. Produced predominantly by the prolific Dallas Austin, the music was utterly contemporary, with crisp beats, synth strings and deep, booming bass complementing the band's pure vocals. The album mixes two distinct styles of songs – funky, hip-hop-influenced pop (as on the first single 'Motownphilly' and 'Little Things') and smooth balladering, such as 'Lonely Heart' and 'It's So Hard To Say Goodbye To Yesterday.'

In 1992, Boyz II Men scored a record-breaking hit with 'The End of the Road', which stayed at the top of the Billboard Hot 100 for a record-breaking 13 weeks. Taken from the soundtrack to the Eddie Murphy film *Boomerang,* the single was added to a reissue of *Cooleyhighharmony* the following year. A Spanish version was also issued, featuring a Spanish-language version of 'The End of the Road', and remixes and radio versions of other songs.

*Cooleyhighharmony* produced three Top 20 singles and secured the Grammy for Best R&B Performance by a Duo or Group With Vocal.

**Number One singles:**
None

**Grammy awards:** Best R&B performance by a duo or group with vocal

**Label:** US: Motown; UK: Polydor

**Recorded in:** N/A

**Personnel:**
Michael McCary
Nathan Morris
Wanya Morris

Shawn Stockman
Jack Bruce
Trilok Gurtu
Mark Nauseef
Dallas Austin
Michael Bivins
Rick Criniti
Jim Hinger
Nakia Keith
Various other personnel

**Producers:**
Dallas Austin
Walter Quintus
Kurt Renker
Mark Nauseef

1 **Please Don't Go** (4:26)
2 **Lonely Heart** (3:42)
3 **This is My Heart** (3:23)
4 **Uhh Ahh** (4:15)
5 **It's So Hard To Say Goodbye To Yesterday** (2:50)
6 **Motownphilly** (3:51)
7 **Under Pressure** (4:14)
8 **Sympin** (4:00)
9 **Little Things** (4:04)
10 **Your Love** (5:51)

Total album length: 40 minutes

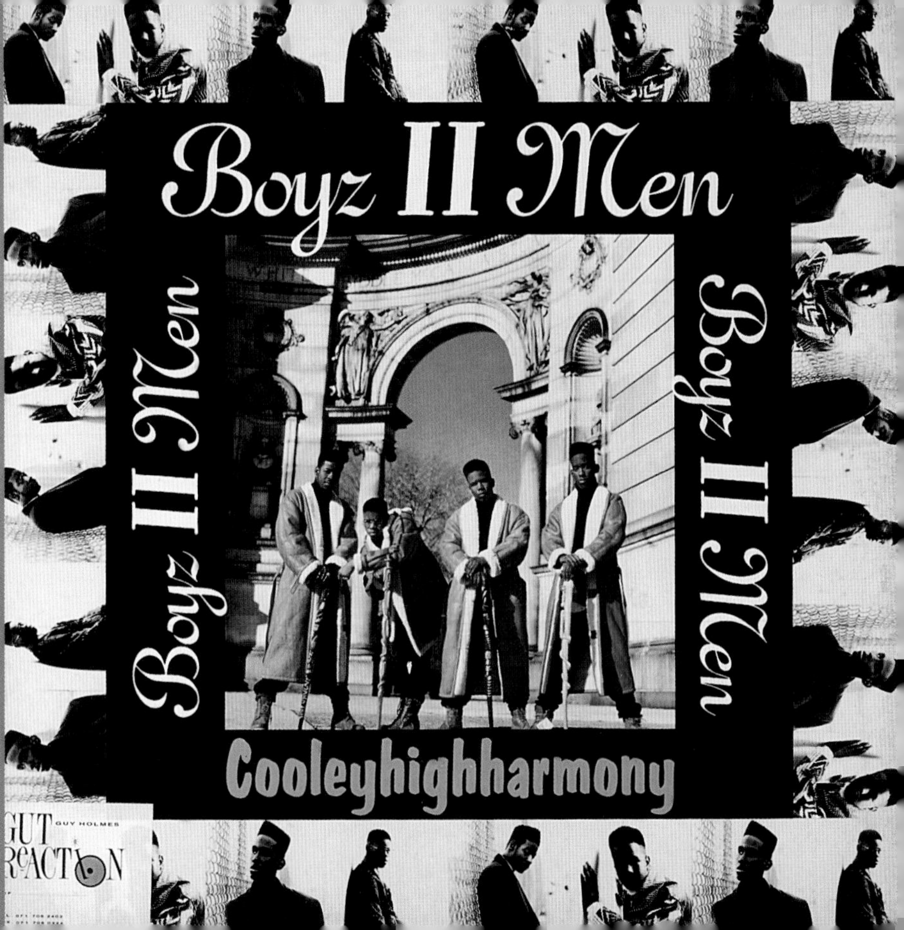


Sleeve artwork by Ulf V. Kanitz

# 44 Some Gave All

| • **Album sales:** 9,100,000 | • **Release date:** May 1992 |

Kentucky-born Billy Ray Cyrus made chart history with his debut album *Some Gave All*, which became the first country album to debut at Number One on the Billboard Hot 100. Although Cyrus's looks made him immediately popular amongst female fans, the album's success was driven by the single 'Achy Breaky Heart', an infectious slice of country pop that became a massive crossover hit, reaching Number Four on the US chart and becoming an airplay favourite.

The rest of the album sees Cyrus tackle both his own material and those by other songwriters,

the deep southern twang and upbeat, soft-rock sound appealing to both country fans and mainstream pop consumers. 'Someday, Somewhere, Somehow' and 'Ain't No Good Goodbye' were traditional tales of heartbreak, 'Never Thought I'd Fall In Love With You' and 'Wher'm I Gonna Live?' had a smooth Eagles-like feel, while 'These Boots Are Made For Walkin'' increased the tempo.

Subsequent single 'Could've Been Me' and 'She's Not Cryin' Anymore' only made Number 72 and Number 70 respectively, but with *Some Gave All* ultimately shifting more than 9,000,000 copies and winning the singer five Grammy nominations, it hardly mattered.

**Number One singles:**
None

**Grammy awards:** None

**Label:** US: Polygram
UK: Mercury

**Recorded in:**
Nashville, USA

**Personnel:**
Billy Ray Cyrus
Clyde Carr
Costo Davis
Greg Fletcher
Sonny Garrish
Keith Hinton
Corky Holbrook
Joe Scaife
Terry Shelton
Barton Stevens

**Producers:**
Jim Cotton
Joe Scaife

1  **Could've Been Me** (3:44)
2  **Achy Breaky Heart** (3:23)
3  **She's Not Cryin' Anymore** (3:25)
4  **Wher'm I Gonna Live?** (3:29)
5  **These Boots Are Made For Walkin'** (2:47)
6  **Someday, Somewhere, Somehow** (3:47)
7  **Never Thought I'd Fall In Love With You** (3:41)
8  **Ain't No Good Goodbye** (3:22)
9  **I'm So Miserable** (3:59)
10 **Some Gave All** (4:05)

Total album length: 36 minutes

# BILLY RAY CYRUS

**SOME**

**GAVE**

**ALL**

# 43 The Sign

| • Album sales: 9,100,000 | • Release date: November 1993 |

Released after the single 'All That She Wants' went platinum and reached Number Two on the Billboard singles chart, *The Sign* was actually a US repackaging of Ace Of Base's debut, *Happy Nation*, with four new songs added. The song's reggae swing, pulsing synths and catchy melody helped make Ace Of Base the first Europop band to break the US market, succeeding where pop pioneers and compatriots ABBA had struggled. As a result, *The Sign* sold an astonishing 9,000,000 copies in the States and became the first Swedish album to top the Billboard Hot 100.

The rest of *The Sign* doesn't really deviate from the formula of its first single, but there's little denying Ulf Ekberg and Jonas Berggren's gift for commercial pop songwriting. The other singles – reggae standard 'Don't Turn Around' and 'Living in Danger' became US Top 40 hits, while 'The Sign' reached Number One. All have a similar reggae bounce, while disco-tinged 'Young And Proud' is designed for the dancefloor. 'Happy Nation' attempts to be slightly edgier, but really this album was an exercise in unashamed pop music. *The Sign* earned the band three Grammy nominasions, including one for Best New Artist.

**Number one singles:**
US: The Sign; UK: All That She Wants

**Grammy awards:** None

**Label:** US: Arista;
UK: London

**Recorded in:** N/A

**Personnel:**
Jonas 'Joker' Berggren
Ulf 'Buddha' Ekberg
Linn Berggren
Jenny Berggren
John Ballard

**Producers:**
The Pop!
Jonas 'Joker' Berggren
Ulf 'Buddha' Ekberg
Stonestream
Tommy Ekman
T.O.E.C.
Adebratt

1 All That She Wants (3:34
2 Don't Turn Around (3:51
3 Young And Proud (3:56
4 The Sign (3:12
5 Living In Danger (3:43
6 Dancer In A Daydream (3:39
7 Wheel Of Fortune (3:54
8 Waiting For Magic (3:53
9 Happy Nation (4:16
10 Voulez-Vous Danser (3:20
11 My Mind (4:11
12 All That She Wants [Banghra Version] (4:16)

Total album length: 43 minutes

# 42 Time, Love & Tenderness

| • **Album sales:** 9,200,000 | • **Release date:** April 1991 |

Everything about *Time, Love & Tenderness* is big – the voice, the production and the record sales. The album saw Bolton moving even further from his hard-rock roots – these were old-fashioned, soul-based love songs delivered in unsubtle but dynamic style.

**Number one singles:**
US: When A Man Loves A Woman

**Grammy awards:** Best male pop vocal performance

**Label:** US & UK: Columbia

**Recorded in:** N/A

**Personnel:**
Michael Bolton
Patti LaBelle
Kenny G
John Beasley
Desmond Child
Michael Thompson
Jeanie Tracy
Larry Batiste
Kitty Beethoven
Terry Brock
Chris Camozzi
Gary Cirimelli
Laura Creamer
Gary Grant
Sandy Griffith
Chris Hawkins
Dan Higgins,
Skyler Jett
Melisa Kary
Michael Landau
Claytoven Richardson
Myriam Naomi Valle
Larry Williams
Joe Lynn Turner
Walter Afanasieff
Randy Jackson
Various other personnel

**Producers:**
Walter Afanasieff
Michael Bolton

Much of the record's success can be attributed to Bolton's choice of writing partners – Desmond Child was the decade's top rock hit merchant, while Diane Warren is one of the most successful female songwriters ever. Other collaborators include Bob Dylan, who co-wrote 'Steel Bars', easy-listening sax man Kenny G on 'Missing You Now' and Patti LaBelle on the duet 'We're Not Makin' Love Anymore'.

Despite reaching the top of the album charts and spawning four Top 20 singles, the album's success was marred by the Isley's Brothers' lawsuit against Bolton, when they successfully argued that 'Love is a Wonderful Thing' plagiarized their 1961 song of the same name.

1 Love Is A Wonderful Thing (4:43)
2 Time, Love And Tenderness (5:31)
3 Missing You Now (4:33)
4 Forever Isn't Long Enough (4:32)
5 Now That I Found You (4:32)
6 When A Man Loves A Woman (3:52)
7 We're Not Makin' Love Anymore (4:41)
8 New Love (4:32)
9 Save Me (4:21)
10 Steel Bars (3:28)

Total album length: 45 minutes

# MICHAEL BOLTON

## TIME, LOVE & TENDERNESS

# 41 Achtung Baby

| • **Album sales:** 9,200,000 | • **Release date:** November 1991 |

With their eighth album, *Achtung Baby*, U2 turned their back on the American rock styles of *The Joshua Tree* and *Rattle And Hum*, retreated to Berlin and produced the most ambitious record of their career. Although this conscious attempt to reinvent their sound wasn't entirely uncompromising, *Achtung Baby* still sold over 9,000,000 copies and contained some of U2's most memorable songs.

*Achtung Baby* was produced by regulars Steve Lillywhite, Daniel Lanois and Brian Eno, the latter being especially key in transforming the band's sound, much as he had with David Bowie on *Low*, *Heroes* and *Lodger* over a decade earlier.

The first single, 'The Fly', was indicative of the band's new sound. The Edge's dirty guitar, Bono's distorted vocals and the pounding, dubby beats producing a startling mix of the melodic and the experimental. 'Zoo Station' and 'Even Better Than The Real Thing' continues the guitar-heavy sound. 'One' and 'Who's Gonna Ride Your Wild Horses' are classic U2 ballads.

*Achtung Baby* entered the Billboard chart at Number One and produced six singles, some with mixed success. 'One' hit the Top Ten in both the UK and US, but the UK chart-topping 'The Fly' only made Number 61 in the US.

---

**Number One singles:**
UK: The Fly

**Grammy awards:** Best rock performance by a duo or group with vocals

**Label:** US & UK: Island

**Recorded in:** Berlin, Germany; Dublin, Ireland

**Personnel:**
Bono
The Edge
Adam Clayton
Larry Mullen
Daniel Lanois
Brian Eno

**Producers:**
Brian Eno
Daniel Lanois
Steve Lillywhite

1 Zoo Station (4:36)
2 Even Better than The Real Thing (3:41)
3 One (4:36)
4 Until The End of the World (4:39)
5 Who's Gonna Ride Your Wild Horses (5:16)
6 So Cruel (5:49)
7 The Fly (4:29)
8 Mysterious Ways (4:04)
9 Tryin' To Throw Your Arms Around the World (3:53)
10 Ultraviolet (Light My Way) (5:31)
11 Acrobat (4:30)
12 Love Is Blindness (4:23)

Total album length: 55 minutes

# **40** Mariah Carey

• Album sales: 9,300,000 | • Release date: May 1990

Mariah Carey's debut album left little doubt that this young woman was going to be a major star. The 20-year-old's incredible voice and the fact that she co-wrote every track on the album made her stand out from the rest of the post-Whitney divas, and despite a slow start, after 36 weeks of release, it reached Number One in the Billboard chart and won two Grammy awards.

A number of different producers took material Carey that had written with song-writing partner Ben Margulies and created a polished, commercial sound; the record combine into emotional, synth-drenched ballads and catchy, upbeat soul-pop, Carey's sweeping vocals dominating all.

Opening track 'Vision Of Love' was Carey's debut single and her first Number One, a ballad with a doo-wop swing on which producer Rhett Lawrence making good use of breathy backing vocals and lush keyboard sounds. The gospel-influenced 'There's Got To Be A Way' and 'Someday' were faster and catchy, while 'You Need Me' has an edgier feel to it.

The album produced four Number Ones – 'Vision of Love', 'Someday', and the ballads 'I Don't Wanna Cry' and 'Love Takes Time'.

**Number One singles:**
US: Vison Of Love; Love Takes Time; Someday; I Don't Wanna Cry

**Grammy awards:** Best new artist; Best female pop vocal performance – Visions Of Love

**Label:** US & UK: Columbia

**Recorded in:**
New York, USA

**Personnel:**
Mariah Carey
Jimmy Rip
Vernon 'Ice' Black
Chris Camozzi
Bob Cadway
Chris Toland

David Williams
Michael Landau
Nile Rodgers
Richard Tee
Walter Afanasieff
Louis Biancaniello
Ben Margulies
Rhett Lawrence
Rich Tancredi
Marcus Miller
Joe Franco
Narada Michael Walden
Omar Hakim
Ren Klyce
Various other personnel

**Producers:**
Ric Wake
Narada Michael Walden
Mariah Carey
Ben Margulies
Walter Afanasieff

1 Vision Of Love (3:30)
2 There's Got To Be A Way (4:53)
3 I Don't Wanna Cry (4:48)
4 Someday (4:08)
5 Vanishing (4:12)
6 All In Your Mind (4:45)
7 Alone In Love (4:12)
8 You Need Me (3:51)
9 Sent From Up Above (4:04)
10 Prisoner (4:24)
11 Love Takes Time (3:49)

Total album length: 46 minutes

# 39 Mellon Collie And The Infinite Sadness

| • Album sales: 9,300,000 | • Release date: October 1995 |

There can be few albums quite so extravagant, in both title and contents, as the Smashing Pumpkin's third album *Mellon Collie and the Infinite Sadness*. Nonetheless, this sprawling yet consistent two-hour listen that proved one of the most successful hard rock albums of the decade.

With 28 songs spread across two discs, singer, songwriter and guitarist Billy Corgan finds plenty of room to explore a variety of rock styles The first disc, subtitled 'Dusk to Dawn', is probably the more direct, with thunderous, anthemic rockers like 'Zero' and 'Bullet With Butterfly Wings' driven by Jimmy Chamberlin's drumming and Corgan's sneering voice.

Disc two, 'Twilight to Starlight', is a much better example of the band's diversity, from the catchy '1979' and the pounding 'Tales Of A Scorched Earth' to acoustic laments like 'Thirty-three' and the melodic 'By Starlight'.

The album entered the Billboard chart at Number One and produced three Top 50 singles. The band earned six Grammy nominations, winning Best hard rock performance for 'Bullet With Butterfly Wings'.

| | |
|---|---|
| **Number One singles:** None | **Personnel:** Billy Corgan James Iha D'Arcy Jimmy Chamberlin Greg Leisz |
| **Grammy awardss:** Best hard rock performance – Bullet With Butterfly Wings | |
| **Label:** US: Virgin; UK: Hut | **Producers:** Alan Moulder Flood Billy Corgan |
| **Recorded in:** Chicago, USA | |

1 Mellon Collie And The Infinite Sadness (2:52)
2 Tonight, Tonight (4:14)
3 Jellybelly (3:01)
4 Zero (2:40)
5 Here Is No Why (3:45)
6 Bullet With Butterfly Wings (4:17)
7 To Forgive (4:16)
8 An Ode To No One (4:50)
9 Love (4:21)
10 Cupid De Locke (2:50)
11 Galapogos (4:46)
12 Muzzle (3:44)
13 Porcelina Of The Vast Oceans (9:21)
14 Take Me Down (2:52)
15 Where Boys Fear To Tread (4:22)
16 Bodies (4:12)
17 Thirty-Three (4:10)
18 In The Arms Of Sleep (4:12)
19 1979 (4:25)
20 Tales Of A Scorched Earth (0 :46)
21 Thru the Eyes Of Ruby (7:38)
22 Stumbleine (2:54)
23 XYU (7:07)
24 We Only Come Out At Night (4:05)
25 Beautiful (4:18)
26 Lily (My One And Only) (3:31)
27 By Starlight (4:48)
28 Farewell And Goodnight (4:22)

Total album length: 122 minutes

**The Smashing Pumpkins**

The Smashing Pumpkins
Mellon Collie and the Infinite Sadness

# 38 Big Willie Style

| • Album sales: 9,600,000 | • Release date: November 1997 |

The first album that Will Smith released under his own name (as opposed to the Fresh Prince), this party rap collection followed hot on the heels of the actor/rapper's hit films *Men In Black* and *Independence Day*. A world away from the dark, controversial brand of gangsta rap favoured by many hip-hop artists of the time, the massive popularity of *Big Willie Style* proved that a lack of profanity and violent imagery was no barrier to mainstream chart success.

*Big Willie Style* has an impressive production line-up keeping the sound upbeat and funky, with squelching bass, clipped guitars, smooth synths and catchy choruses. Cameo's Larry Blackmon features on an updating of his band's hit 'Candy', while the late Lisa 'Left Eye' Lopes guests on the title track. Smith is a more than capable rapper, the charm and humour of his screen persona transferring to his rhymes.

*Big Willie Style* produced two Number One singles, 'Gettin' Jiggy Wit It' and 'Men In Black', while 'Miami' peaked at Number 17. A new version of Bill Wither's 'Just The Two Of Us', which Smith sings to his son, reached Number 20.

**Number One singles:**
UK: Men In Black; US: Gettin' Jiggy Wit It

**Grammy awards:** Best rap solo performance

**Label:** US: Sony UK: Columbia

**Recorded in:** N/A

**Personnel:**
Will Smith
Larry Blackmon
Fuzzy
Ryan Toby
Valvin Roane
Tia Mintze
'Left Eye' Lopes (d. 2002)

Camp Lo
Sauce
David Foreman
Timothy 'Tyme' Riley
Keith Winfiel,
Lanar 'Kern' Brantley
Rob Chiarelli
L E S
DJ Jazzy Jeff
Kenny Greene
Trey Lorenz
Tricia Covington
Various other personnel

**Producers:**
Poke And Tone
Andreo Heard
L E S
Jeff Townes
Keith Pelzer

1  Intro (1:51)
2  Y'all Know (3:57)
3  Gettin' Jiggy Wit It (3:47)
4  Candy (3:56)
5  Chasing Forever (4:15)
6  Keith B-Real I (1:07)
7  Don't Say Nothin' (4:22)
8  Miami (3:17)
9  Yes Yes Y'all (4:23)
10  I Loved You (4:12)

11  Keith B-Real II (0:30)
12  It's All Good (4:04)
13  Just The Two Of Us (5:15)
14  Keith B-Real III (1:54)
15  Big Willie Style (3:35)
16  Men In Black (3:47)

Total album length: 54 minutes

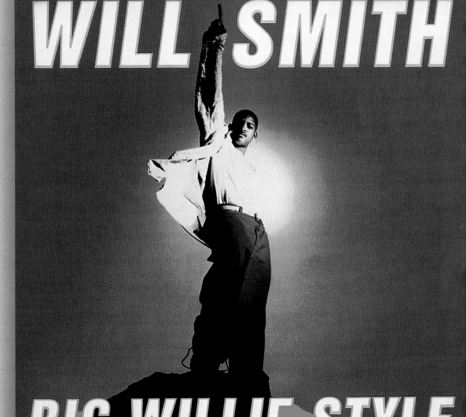

# 37 Spice

• **Album sales:** 10,000,000 | • **Release date:** February 1997

The Spice Girls were one of the biggest pop phenomenons of the 1990s. The five lively English girls topped the Billboard chart with their debut single 'Wannabe', which was followed by two further chart toppers, and became the first group ever to enter the UK chart at Number One. With their debut album, they coined the phrase 'girl power', a catchphrase of late 1990s UK pop.

*Spice* is a classic pop album – just 35 minutes long, the addictive, ubiquitous nature of the singles far outweighing any quality lapses elsewhere.

'Wannabe' introduced the five girls to the world, giving each a turn on the mike and name-checking each one in a rap half-way through. With the exception of Mel C, none of the girls had particularly strong voices, but their relentless energy and enthusiasm more than compensated. 'Say You'll Be There' and the disco-tinged, horn driven 'Who Do You Think You Are' are more sophisticated, funky slices of dance pop, while '2 Become 1' and 'Mama' are classy ballads.

Throughout the album, the girls stress their camaraderie and independence, and this can be seen in the writing credits, where the band wisely ensured their share of royalties by insisting they were co-credited on each song.

| Number One singles: | Emma Bunton |
| --- | --- |
| US & UK: Wannabe | Victoria Adams |
| UK: Say You'll Be There; | Judd Lander |
| 2 Become 1; Who Do You | Pete Davis |
| Think You Are | Judd Lander |
| | Matt Rowe |
| **Grammy awards:** None | Richard Stannard |
| | Paul Waller |
| **Label:** US & UK: Virgin | Mary Pearce |
| | Greg Lester |
| **Recorded in:** N/A | Various other personnel |

| Personnel: | Producers: |
| --- | --- |
| Geri Halliwell | Richard Stannard |
| Melanie B | Matt Rowe |
| Melanie C | Absolute |

1 **Wannabe** (2:52)
2 **Say You'll Be There** (3:56)
3 **2 Become 1** (4:00)
4 **Love Thing** (3:37)
5 **Last Time Lover** (4:11)
6 **Mama** (5:03)
7 **Who Do You Think You Are** (3:59)
8 **Something Kinda Funny** (4:02)
9 **Naked** (4:25)
10 **If U Can't Dance** (3:58)

Total album length: 35 minutes

The Spice Girls

GIRLS

# 36 Life after Death

| • Album sales: 10,000,000 | • Release date: March 1997 |

Biggie Smalls (The Notorious B.I.G)'s murder barely three weeks before this album arrived in the shops may have made him more famous than he ever was when he was alive.

**Number One singles:**
US: Hypnotize; Mo Money
Mo Problems

**Grammy awards:** None

**Label:** US: Bad Boy
UK: Arista

**Recorded in:**
New York, USA

**Personnel:**
Notorious B.I.G (d. 1997)
Jay-Z
The Lox
Too Short
Layzie Bone
Krayzie Bon,
Bizzy Bone
Lil' Kim
Puff Daddy
Daron Jone
112
R Kelly

Carl Thomas
Angela Winbush
Quinnes Parker
Michael Keith
Marvin Scandrick
Carlos 'July Six' Broady
Stevie J
Paragon
Deric 'D-dot' Angelettie
Faith Evans
Pam Long
Kelly Price
Various other personnel

**Producer:**
Sean 'Puffy' Combs
Stevie J
Easy Mo Bee
Daron Jones
Kay-Gee
RZA
Buck-Wild
DJ Premier
Havoc
Clark Kent

Nevertheless, *Life after Death* proved a vital album in the evolution of hip hop, and was a fitting epitaph for this talented rapper.

*Life After Death* comfortably straddled the commercial middle ground of slick, catchy pop rap and the uncompromising, expletive-strewn world of gangsta rap. The album's commercial success was in no way limited to the US. The two American chart toppers, 'Hypnotize' and 'Mo Money Mo Problems', also achieved significant sales in the UK, reaching Number 10 and Number Six, respectively.

1 Life After Death Intro (1:40)
2 Somebody's Gotta Die (4:26)
3 Hypnotize (3:49)
4 Kick In The Door (4:46)
5 #! *@ You Tonight (5:45)
6 Last Day (4:18)
7 I Love The Dough (5:12)
8 What's Beef? (5:15)
9 B I G Interlude (0:48)
10 Mo Money Mo Problems (4:17)
11 Niggas Bleed (4:51)
12 I Got A Story To Tell (4:42)
13 Notorious Thugs (6:07)
14 Miss U (4:59)
15 Another (4:15)
16 Going Back To Cali (5:07)
17 Ten Crack Commandments (3:24)
18 Playa Hater (3:57)
19 Nasty Boy (5:33)
20 Sky's The Limit (5:29)
21 The World Is Filled... (4:54)
22 My Downfall (5:26)
23 Long Kiss Goodnight (5:18)
24 You're Nobody (Til Somebody Kills You) (4:53)

Total album length: 109 minutes

# 35 Human Clay

| • **Album sales:** 10,000,000 | • **Release date:** September 1999 |

Even with the grunge explosion over, and nu-metal beginning to capture the imagination of America's youth, Creed proved that well-crafted, traditional heavy rock could still sell. *Human Clay*, Creed's second album, outsold their debut, and entered the Billboard album chart at Number One. What's more, the single 'With Arms Wide Open' topped the US singles chart, reached Number Three in the UK, and won the band a Grammy in 2000 for Best Rock Song.

Produced by John Philip Kurzweg, *Human Clay* puts the emphasis on Mark Tremonti's crunching riffs and singer Scott Stapp's passionate vocals. The band was heavily influenced by Seattle bands such as

Soundgarden and Alice in Chains, who had, in turn, taken their lead from classic rock outfits such as Black Sabbath and Led Zeppelin.

There's no denying that the songwriting here is of a very high standard. 'Are You Ready?', 'What If' and 'Beautiful' are straight-forward grinding rockers, 'Higher' and 'Inside Us All' are surprisingly melodic, the dark 'Wrong Way' throws some Eastern scales into the mix, while 'Faceless Man' and the massive single 'With Arms Wide Open' reveal a softer, more introspective side to the band.

---

**Number One singles:**
US: With Arms Wide Open

**Grammy awards:** Best Rock Song – With Arms Wide Open

**Label:** US & UK: Epic

**Recorded in:**
Tallahassee, USA

**Personnel:**
Scott Stapp
Mark Tremonti
Brian Marshall
Scott Phillips

**Producer:**
John Philip Kurzweg

1 Are You Ready? (4:45)
2 What If (5:18)
3 Beautiful (4:19)
4 Say I (5:15)
5 Wrong Way (4:19)
6 Faceless Man (5:58)
7 Never Die (4:51)
8 With Arms Wide Open (4:34)
9 Higher (5:16)
10 Wash Away Those Years (6:04)
11 Inside Us All (5:39)

Total album length: 56 minutes

Creed

# CREED

## human clay

# 34 Fly

| • Album sales: 10,000,000 | • Release date: October 1999 |

The second album to feature vocalist Natalie Maines, *Fly* was the Dixie Chicks's follow-up to *Wide Open Spaces*, one of the biggest-selling country albums of all time. This album follows in much the same vein, spirited country-pop mixed with twanging laments. Recorded in the Chick's hometown of Nashville, Tennessee, the album features a large number of studio musicians – including Maines's father, guitar legend Lloyd Maines – but producers Blake Chancey and Paul Worley always ensure that the three leading ladies are to the fore.

*Fly* also saw the band taking a much greater role in writing process, and the album is marked by themes of female empowerment – 'Goodbye Earl' tells of an abused wife getting revenge, 'Sin Wagon' sees its narrator leaving a bored relationship, while the title of 'If I Fall You're Going Down With Me' speaks for itself. The album produced no less than six singles, and triumphed at the 2000 Grammys, winning four nominations and two awards.

**Number One singles:**
None

**Grammy awards:** Best country performance by a duo or group with vocal – Ready To Run; Best country album

**Label:** US: Monument; UK: Epic

**Recorded in:**
Nashville, USA

**Personnel:**
Natalie Maines
Emily Robison
Martie Seide
Paul Worley
Randy Scruggs
Billy Joe Walker Jr
Adam Steinberg
Bryan Sutton
Dennis Linde
Marcus Hummon
Pat Buchanan
George Marinelli
Mike Henderson
Keith Urban
Lloyd Maines
John Mock
Steve Conn
Steve Nathan
Matt Rollings
Michael Rhodes
Greg Morrow
Tom Roady
Terry McMillan
Blake Chancey
Charlie Robison

**Producers:**
Blake Chancey
Paul Worley

1  Ready To Run (3:52)
2  If I Fall You're Going Down With Me (3:05)
3  Cowboy Take Me Away (4:51)
4  Cold Day In July (5:12)
5  Goodbye Earl (4:19)
6  Hello Mr Heartache (3:49)
7  Don't Waste Your Heart (2:49)
8  Sin Wagon (3:41)
9  Without You (3:32)
10  Some Days You Gotta Dance (2:30)
11  Hole In My Head (3:22)
12  Heartbreak Town (3:48)
13 - [Silence] (0:06)
14  Let Him Fly (3:07)

Total album length: 47 minutes

Dixie Chicks

# 33 Dookie

• **Album sales:** 10,300,000 | • **Release date:** February 1994

Green Day were the band that made melodic punk rock a commercial force once again, and *Dookie* sits just behind *Nevermind* in terms of sales and influence. The album is cleanly produced by Rob Cavallo and has a very simple formula: loud, snotty, catchy three-minute punk-pop anthems delivered with a sneer and a smile.

Singer, guitarist and songwriter Billie Joe Armstrong proved to have a great gift for writing a yearning melody and sings about experiences that his young audience could relate to. There is adolescent boredom ('Burnout', 'Longview'), teenage rebellion ('Having A Blast'), messy relationships ('Pulling Teeth'), and smoking pot ('Basket Case'). Musically, Green Day are entirely indebted to the likes of the Buzzcocks and the Jam, with flashes of ska ('When I Come Around)' thrown in for good measure.

*Dookie* rode in on the massive success of first single 'Longview', which may not have made much of an impact on the Billboard charts, but was granted massive exposure on mainstream rock radio and on MTV, as were subsequent singles 'Basket Case' and 'When I Come Around'. The album itself reached Number Two on the Billboard album chart, and took the Grammy award for Best Alternative Music Performance in 1995.

| | |
|---|---|
| **Number One singles:** none | **Personnel:** Billie Joe Armstrong Mike Dirnt Tre Cool |
| **Grammy awards:** Best alternative music performance | |
| **Label:** US & UK: Reprise | **Producer:** Rob Cavallo Billie Joe Armstrong Mike Dirnt Tre Cool |
| **Recorded in:** N/A | |

1 Burnout (2:07)
2 Having A Blast (2:44)
3 Chump (2:54)
4 Longview (3:59)
5 Welcome To Paradise (3:44)
6 Pulling Teeth (2:30)
7 Basket Case (3:03)
8 She (2:14)
9 Sassafras Roots (2:37)
10 When I Come Around (2:58)
11 Coming Clean (1:34)
12 Emenius (1:43)
13 In The End (1:46)
14 F.O.D./All By Myself (5:46)

Total album length: 40 minutes

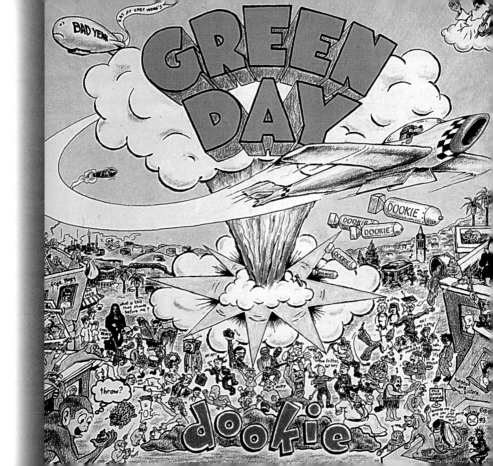

# 32 The Lion King

| • **Album sales:** 10,300,000 | • **Release date:** July 1994 |

Disney's blockbuster animated film *The Lion King* produced the decade's second biggest selling soundtrack album. Although it is best known for composer Elton John and lyricist Tim Rice's contributions, the orchestral work of Hans Zimmer was equally well represented.

The soundtrack opens with five John/Rice songs from the movie itself, which saw John weaving African rhythms and melodies into the more traditional Disney format. There's the epic theme song 'The Circle Of Life', the lively 'I Just Can't Wait To Be King', the percussion-heavy, Jeremy Irons-voiced 'Be Prepared', the off-beat 'Hakuna Mata' and the love song 'Can You Feel The Love Tonight?' The quartet of Hans Zimmer's pieces are equally evocative of the African theme.

The album closes with Elton John's own versions of three of his film songs. Ironically – in that John doesn't sing in the film itself – two of these, 'Circle Of Life' and 'Can You Feel The Love Tonight?', were successful singles, the latter reaching Number Four on the Billboard chart.

**Number One singles:**
None

**Grammy awards:**
Best male pop vocal performance; Best musical album For children

**Label:** US: Disney
UK: Rocket

**Recorded in:** Los Angeles, USA; London, UK; Mmabatho, South Africa

**Personnel:**
Elton John
Kiki Dee
Richard Harvey
Jeremy Irons
Whoopi Goldberg

Jim Cumming
Sally Dworsky
Mbongeni Ngema
Chuck Sabo
Phil Spalding
Carmen Twillie
Laura Williams
Jason Weaver
Nathan Lane
Ernie Sabella
Rowan Atkinson
Gary Barlow
Joseph Williams
David Johnston
Various other personnel

**Producers:**
Hans Zimmer
Mark Mancina
Jay Rifkin
Chris Thomas

1 The Circle Of Life (3:53)
2 I Just Can't Wait To Be King (2:49)
3 Be Prepared (3:38)
4 Hakuna Mata (3:31)
5 Can You Feel The Love Tonight? (2:56)
6 This Land (2:53)
7 To Die For (4:16)
8 Under The Stars (3:42)
9 King Of Pride Rock (5:56)
10 The Circle Of Life (4:49)
11 I Just Can't Wait To Be King (3:35)
12 Can You Feel The Love Tonight? (3:59)

Total album length: 46 minutes

Walt Disney Pictures
Presents

# THE
# LION KING

Original Songs
Music *by* Elton John
Lyrics *by* Tim Rice

Score Composed *by* Hans Zimmer

# SPECIAL EDITION

# Tragic Kingdom

| • **Album sales:** 10,300,000 | • **Release date:** October 1995 |

No Doubt's self-titled major label debut, released in 1992, had failed to chart, so when *Tragic Kingdom* didn't initially make much impact, the band may have not been that surprised. However, the strength of the singles on this third album eventually turned their fortunes around, giving No Doubt a Number One smash and returning the new wave/ska sound of the early 1980s to the mainstream.

*Tragic Kingdom* was produced by Matthew Wilder – who had himself scored a new-wave hit with 'Break My Stride' in 1983. Llike the best rock producers of the 1990s, Wilder emphasised both the band's pop sensibilities and their guitar edge. Songs like 'Different People', 'You Can Do It' and Top-30 singles 'Spiderwebs' and 'Just a Girl' were fast-paced, addictive slices of ska/power-pop marked by Gwen Stefani's alternatively girlish and attitude-filled vocals. The songs were also supported by the ultra-tight rhythm section of bassist Tony Kanal and drummer Adrian Young.

However, it was the third single 'Don't Speak' that proved the album's defining moment. An old-fashioned power ballad detailing the break-up of Stefani and Kanal's relationship, it became the band's first Number One, their biggest-selling single and secured two Grammy nominations.

**Number One singles:**
UK: Don't Speak

**Grammy awards:** None

**Label:** US & UK:
Interscope

**Recorded in:** N/A

**Personnel:**
Gwen Stefani
Tom Dumont
Eric Stefani
Tony Kanal
Adrian Young
Aloke DasGupta
Melissa Hasin
Gerard Boisse
Bill Bergman
Greg Smith
Phil Jordan
Les Lovitt
Nick Lane
Gabe McNair
Matthew Wilder
Stephen Perkins

**Producer:**
Matthew Wilder

1  **Spiderwebs**  (4:28)
2  **Excuse Me Mr**  (3:04)
3  **Just A Girl**  (3:29)
4  **Happy Now?**  (3:43)
5  **Different People**  (4:34)
6  **Hey You**  (3:34)
7  **The Climb**  (6:37)
8  **Sixteen**  (3:21)
9  **Sunday Morning**  (4:33)
10  **Don't Speak**  (4:23)
11  **You Can Do It**  (4:13)
12  **World Go 'Round**  (4:09)
13  **End It on This**  (3:45)
14  **Tragic Kingdom**  (5:31)

Total album length: 59 minutes

**No Doubt**

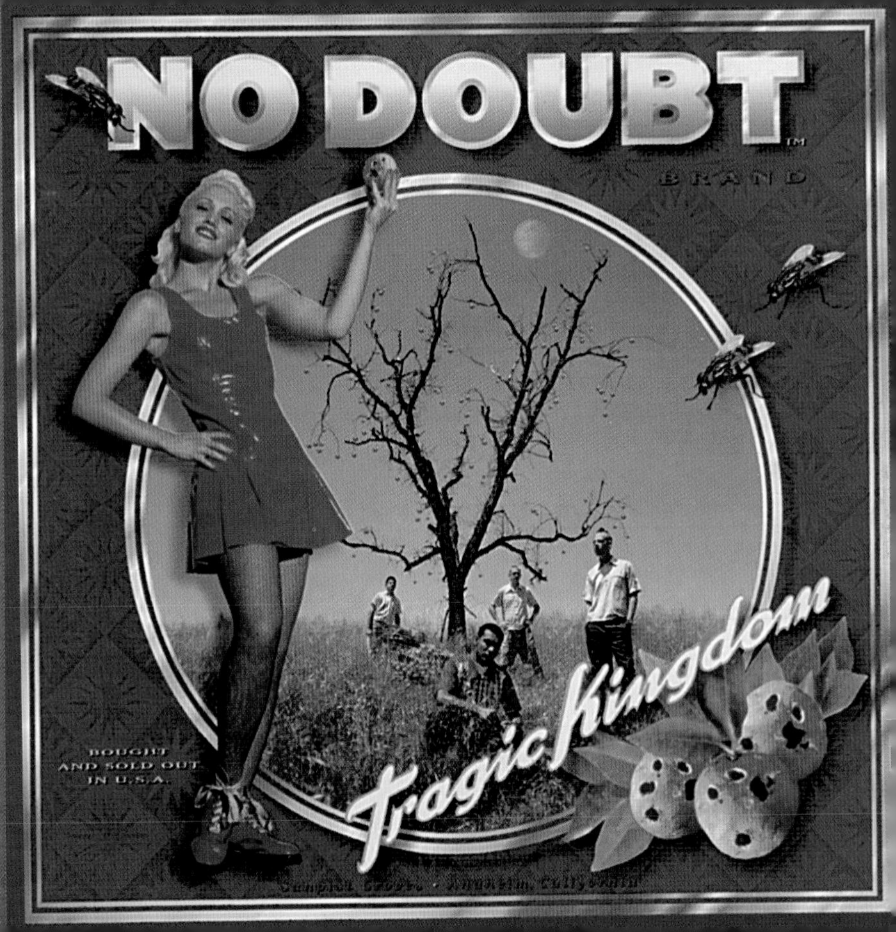
NO DOUBT™
BRAND
BOUGHT
AND SOLD OUT
IN U.S.A.
Tragic Kingdom

# 30 Please Hammer, Don't Hurt 'Em

| • **Album sales:** 10,600,000 | • **Release date:** February 1990 |

Through-out the 1980s hip-hop had seemed to be the most credible of musical genres, but all that changed when *Please Hammer, Don't Hurt 'Em* became the biggest album of 1990 – and the biggest selling rap album of all time. Critics and rap aficionados may have been less than enthusiastic, but MC Hammer's clean-cut image, wholesale lifting from a variety of soul/funk sources and undeniable pop sensibilities helped make hip-hop into a mainstream phenomenon.

'U Can't Touch This' was the song that introduced Hammer to the world, it's smart appropriation of Rick James's 'Super Freak' making the song a massive seller; only the fact it was just available as a 12-inch single stopped it from reaching Number One. The album's other singles proved equally lucrative, if equally reliant on their source material. 'Pray', which sampled Prince's 'When Dove's Cry' reached Number Two, while his version of the Chi-Lite's 1971 hit 'Have You Seen Her' reached Number Four.

With its fat beats, horn samples, whooping female backing vocals and innumerable self-references, the rest of the album followed in much the same vein of slick party hip-hop, giving the world its first rap superstar.

**Number One singles:**
None

**Grammy awards:** Best R&B song; Best rap solo performance; Best music video, long form

**Label:** US & UK: Capitol

**Recorded in:** N/A

**Personnel:**
MC Hammer
Ho Frat Ho!
James Early
The Lone Mixe
Felton Pilot
DJ Redeemed
Soft Touch
Sweet Linda Divine
Too Big MC
Sweet L D

**Producers:**
Felton Pilot
MC Hammer
James Early

1 Here Comes The Hammer (4:32)
2 U Can't Touch This (4:17)
3 Have You Seen Her? (4:42)
4 Yo!! Sweetness (4:36)
5 Help The Children (5:17)
6 On Your Face (4:32)
7 Dancing Machine (2:55)
8 Pray (5:13)
9 Crime Story (5:09)
10 She's Soft And Wet (3:25)
11 Black Is Black (4:31)
12 Let's Go Deeper (5:16)
13 Work This (5:03)

Total album length: 59 minutes

# 29 Nevermind

• Album sales: 10,600,000 • Release date: September 1991

The single most important rock album of the 1990s, *Nevermind* opened the door for dozens of similarly angst-ridden bands from Seattle and sounded the death knell for the commercial glam-metal movement and power ballads of the previous decade. The album sold over 10,000,000 copies worldwide and made lead singer/guitarist Kurt Cobain a massive, if sometimes, reluctant rock icon.

While Cobain's lyrics were unquestionably powerful and heartfelt, the true success of *Nevermind* came from the music. Butch Vig managed to make the band sound both slick and raw at the same time – this was an expensively produced album on a major label, but it was also loud, brash and sounded very real.

The words may have been uncompromising, but the tunes were not – genre-defining songs such as 'Smells Like Teen Spirit', 'Come as You Are', 'Lithium' or 'On A Plain' have classic rock structures, enabled by Krist Novoselic and Dave Grohl's powerhouse rhythm section and Cobain's vocal roar. It wasn't all pedal-to-the-metal stuff – 'Polly' is a chilling acoustic tale of kidnap and the closing 'Something In The Way' is marked by Kirk Canning's mournful cello – but as a blast of pure punk rock energy, *Nevermind* has had few rivals before or since.

**Number One singles:**
None

**Grammy awards:** None

**Label:** US & UK: Geffen

**Recorded in:**
Van Nuys, USA

**Personnel:**
Kurt Cobain (d. 1994)
Krist Novoselic
Dave Grohl
Kirk Canning

**Producer:**
Butch Vig

1  Smells Like Teen Spirit  (5:02)
2  In Bloom  (4:15)
3  Come As You Are  (3:39)
4  Breed  (3:04)
5  Lithium  (4:17)
6  Polly  (2:56)
7  Territorial Pissings  (2:23)
8  Drain You  (3:44)
9  Lounge Act  (2:37)
10  Stay Away  (3:33)
11  On A Plain  (3:17)
12  Something In The Way  (3:51)

Total album length: 42 minutes

NIRVANA
NEVERMIND

# 28 Daydream

• **Album sales:** 10,600,000 • **Release date:** October 1995

Mariah Carey's fourth album was probably the most successful at combining the three elements that made her the biggest-selling female artist of the decade: her amazing five-octave voice, the ballads for which she was well known, and the emerging R&B sound that would mark her subsequent releases.

Lead-off track 'Fantasy' became the first single by a female artist ever to debut at Number One on the Hot 100. It marked a new sound for Carey, her voice riding on top of a sample of Tom Tom Club's 'Genius of Love' and an infectious multi-tracked chorus. 'Always Be My Baby' had a 1960s pop feel, 'Long Ago' continued the more beat-orientated sound, while 'One Sweet Day' (which spent a record-breaking 16 weeks at Number One) saw Carey team up with Boyz II Men, the biggest R&B group of the day.

Of course, it's the ballads to which her voice has always been best-suited and the likes of the dreamy 'Underneath The Stars', 'I Am Free' and the Journey cover 'Open Arms' are classic Carey.

**Number One singles:**
US: Fantasy; One Sweet Day; Always Be My Baby

**Grammy awards:** None

**Label:** US & UK: Columbia

**Recorded in:** N/A

**Personnel:**
Mariah Carey
Shawn Stockman
Michael S McCary
Nathan Morris
Wanya Morris
Dave 'Jam' Hall
Jermaine Dupri
Manuel Sea
Dann Huff
Tristan Avakian
Terry Barrus
Lori Holland
Babyface
Walter Afanasieff
David Morales
Satoshi Tomiie
Dan Shea
Steve Thornton
Gary Cirimelli
Randy Walker
Kelly Price
Melonie Daniels
Shanrae Price

**Producers:**
David Hall
Walter Afanasieff
Mariah Carey
Jermaine Dupri
David Morales

1 Fantasy (4:04)
2 Underneath The Stars (3:33)
3 One Sweet Day (4:42)
4 Open Arms (3:30)
5 Always Be My Baby (4:20)
6 I Am Free (3:09)
7 When I Saw You (4:24)
8 Long Ago (4:33)
9 Melt Away (3:42)
10 Forever (4:00)
11 Daydream Interlude (3:04)
12 Looking In (3:35)

Total album length: 47 minutes

# 27 Unplugged

| • **Album sales:** 10,900,000 | • **Release date:** August 1992 |

MTV's series of Unplugged live-in-the-studio shows produced a number of notable releases during the nineties, but Eric Clapton's was the biggest selling, and one of the best. The album saw Clapton returning to his blues roots, mixing up reinterpreted classics from his back catalogue with blues standards.

Clapton works a with small, tight band – bass, drums, some light keyboards – and the emphasis is on his voice and guitar work. The album opens with the Latino-inflected instrumental 'Signe', before moving into a version of Bo Diddley's

'Before You Accuse Me'. Clapton shows the depth his blues passion by reviving the likes of Jimmy Cox's 'Nobody Knows You When You're Down And Out', Robert Johnson's 'Walkin' Blues' and Jesse Fuller's 'San Francisco Bay Blues'.

However, it's Clapton's own material that makes *Unplugged* one of his most important albums. Clapton breathes new life into 'Layla' by giving it a ragtime swagger, while 'Tears In Heaven' is a heartbreaking dedication to Clapton's late son Conor. *Unplugged* won five Grammys and hit Number One on the Billboard chart.

**Number One singles:**
None

**Grammy awards:** Record of the year; Album of the year; Song of the year; best male pop vocal performance; Best male rock vocal performance; Best rock song

**Label:** US & UK: Warners

**Recorded in:**
Berkshire, UK

**Personnel:**
Eric Clapton,
Chuck Leavel
Nathan East
Steve Ferrone
Ray Cooper
Katy Kissoon
Tessa Niles

**Producer:**
Russ Titelman

1  Signe (3:13)
2  Before You Accuse Me (3:44)
3  Hey Hey (3:16)
4  Tears In Heaven (4:36)
5  Lonely Stranger (5:27)
6  Nobody Knows You When You're Down and Out (3:49)
7  Layla (4:46)
8  Running On Faith (6:30)
9  Walkin' Blues (3:37)
10 Alberta (3:42)
11 San Francisco Bay Blues (3:23)
12 Malted Milk (3:36)
13 Old Love (7:52)
14 Rollin' And Tumblin' (4:12)

Total album length: 62 minutes

eric **clapton** unplugged

# 26 Pieces Of You

| • Album sales: 11,000,000 | • Release date: February 1995 |

Jewel Kilcher was musically inclined from childhood, having performed alongside her parents from the age of six, and to a certain extent the 21-year-old's debut is the 'story so far' of a young woman's burgeoning talent.

Jewel began her professional career in a San Diego coffee shop called the Innerchange where she slowly developed a devoted following at her regular Thursday night slots. By this time she was performing new material every week, although some of the songs to be featured on *Pieces of You* were written during her high school years. Inevitably, word spread within the music industry, and she was signed to Atlantic Records in 1994.

Producer Ben Keith was personally chosen by Jewel, who was looking for someone who would allow her talents to mature naturally. A sound crew recorded a number of live tracks at the Innerchange in July for inclusion on the album. Other tracks were recorded at Neil Young's Broken Arrow Ranch studio.

*Pieces Of You* was expected to sell around 30–40,000 copies and sales were indeed slow following its release. It wasn't until 14 months after the album's release that *Pieces Of You* entered the Billboard Top 200, bouyed by the popularity of the hit 'Who Will Save Your Soul'. After aggressive promotion and an exhausting tour, the album started to sell massively, eventually securing 11 platinums – an impressive feat for the debut from a female solo artist.

| Number One singles: | Personnel: |
| --- | --- |
| None | Jewel Kilcher |
| | Kris Wilkinson |
| Grammy awards: | Robbie Buchanan |
| None | Charlotte Caffey |
| | Spooner Oldham |
| Label: US & UK: Atlantic | Tim Drummond |
| | Mark Howard |
| Recorded in: Woodside & San Diego, USA | Oscar Butterworth |
| | Producer: Ben Keith |

1 Who Will Save Your Soul (4:00)
2 Pieces Of You (4:15)
3 Little Sister (2:29)
4 Foolish Games (5:39)
5 Near You Always (3:08)
6 Painters (6:43)
7 Morning Song (3:35)
8 Adrian (7:02)
9 I'm Sensitive (2:54)
10 You Were Meant For Me (4:13)
11 Don't (3:34)
12 Daddy (3:49)
13 Angel Standing By (2:38)
14 Amen 4:32

Total album length: 59 minutes

*Jewel*

pieces of you

what we call human nature in actuality is human habit

# 25 Devil Without a Cause

| • **Album sales:** 11,000,000 | • **Release date:** August 1998 |

Crafty style surfer and purveyor of white trash sensibilities, Kid Rock pleased all parties and disaffected none with this raucous blend of hard rock and hip-hop. The confident riffing was the perfect setting for Rock's lyrical bombast as he delivers his own concoction of arrogant streetwise, but self-knowing rap.

That this record exists at all is quite remarkable considering the fortunes that met Kid Rock on his journey through the nineties. He had been treading the margins of success for ten years releasing relatively unnoticed albums. His ultimate success can be put down to sheer perseverance and the fortunate and timely emergence of rap metal.

Rock adds his distinctive personality to a host of heavy rock riffs, including the opener and Grammy-nominated 'Bawitdaba', 'I am the Bullgod' and 'Cowboy'. Fellow white rapper Eminem gets a credit on 'F-ck Off'.

Kid Rock's eclectic mix of styles, drawn from sources as diverse as the Beastie Boys and Lynyrd Skynyrd, gelled in the late 1990s, but his own skill as a lyricist shouldn't be overlooked.

**Number One singles:**
None

**Grammy awards:** None

**Label:** US & UK: Lava-Atlantic

**Recorded in:**
Detroit, USA

**Personnel:**
Kid Rock
Twisted Brown Trucker
Joe C
Kenny Olson
Jason Krause
Jimmy Bones
Stefanie Eulinberg
Kracker
Misty Love
Shirley Hayden

**Producers:**
John Travis
Kid Rock

1　Bawitdaba (4:27)
2　Cowboy (4:17)
3　Devil Without a Cause (5:32)
4　I Am the Bullgod (4:50)
5　Roving Gangster (Rollin') (4:24)
6　Wasting Time (4:02)
7　Welcome 2 the Party (Ode 2 the Old School) (5:14)
8　I Got One for Ya (3:43)
9　Somebody's Gotta Feel This (3:08)
10　Fist of Rage (3:23)
11　Only God Knows Why (5:27)
12　F-ck Off (6:13)
13　Where U at Rock (4:24)
14　Black Chick, White Guy (12:01)

Total album length: 72 minutes

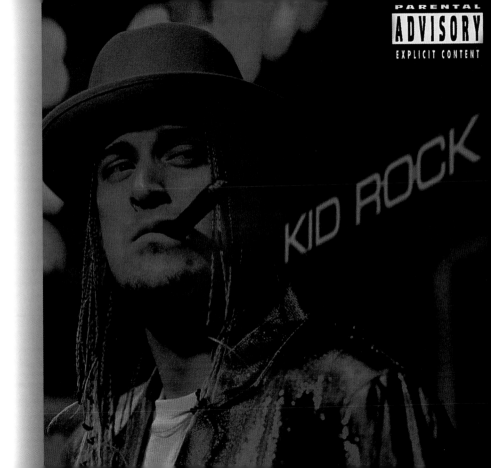

# 24 CrazySexyCool

• **Album sales:** 11,300,000 | • **Release date:** November 1994 |

Prince is a good starting point for anybody wanting to know where this album is coming from. Not only do TLC cover – and redefine – his 1987 hit 'If I Was Your Girlfriend', the whole album is imbued with slinky, sexy mid-paced soul and funk very much in the Prince tradition. At the cutting edge but also accessible, *CrazySexyCool* is brimming with feel-good sensuous sounds.

The stand-out track is the delightfully insistent 'Waterfalls', which went on to spend seven weeks at the top of the US charts. With its deft arrangement and catchy chorus, 'Waterfalls' established itself as one of the classic dance tracks of its era. Close behind come two more singles 'Creep' and 'Red Light Special'.

The immense popularity of the trio – Tionne Watkins, Rozonda Thomas and Lisa 'Left Eye' Lopes – was aided by their exuberant style and spirit, and a penchant for stunning costumes. Also key to their success was their choice of collaborators, including Babyface. Tragically Lisa 'Left-Eye' Lopes was killed in an automobile accident in April 2002.

**Number One singles:**
US: Creep

**Grammy awards:** Best R&B album; Best R&B performance by a duo or group with vocals

**Label:** US: La Face; UK: Arista

**Recorded in:**
Various locations, USA

**Personnel:**
Tionne 'T-Boz' Watkins
Lisa 'Left Eye' Lopes (d. 2002)
Rozonda 'Chilli' Thomas

**Producers:**
Dallas Austin
Jermaine Dupri
Babyface
Chucky Thompson

1   Intro-Lude  (1:01)
2   Creep  (4:29)
3   Kick Your Game  (4:13)
4   Diggin' On You  (4:14)
5   Case Of The Fake People  (4:03)
6   Crazysexycool-Interlude  (1:42)
7   Red Light Special  (5:02)
8   Waterfalls  (4:39)
9   Intermission-Lude  (0:42)
10  Let's Do It Again  (4:17)
11  If I Was Your Girlfriend  (4:43)
12  Sexy-Interlude  (1:35)
13  Take Our Time  (4:33)
14  Can I Get A Witness (Interlude)  (2:57)
15  Switch  (3:30)
16  Sumthin' Wicked This Way Comes  (4:30)

Total album length: 56 minutes

TLC

# 23 Music Box

• **Album sales:** 11,500,000 • **Release date:** August 1993

Mariah Carey's third studio album marked a return to the top of the US album chart, a position she held for eight weeks. Much accused of 'over singing', on *Music Box* Carey was clearly at pains to prove that she was capable of at least partial restraint. Her vocal pyrotechnics do inevitably – and quite rightly – explode from time to time, but she and songwriting partner Walter Afanasieff produce a cohesive and, by her standards, more understated affair than usual.

The more measured approach did little to dampen the interest of fans and her scale-vaulting prowess emerges unscathed on the big hits – 'Hero' and 'Dreamlover' – where her emotive side is very much to the fore. In fact, this release turned out to be the best-selling album to date for the best-selling female artist of the 1990s.

Obvious comparisons have been drawn between Carey, Whitney Houston and Celine Dion, all immensely gifted divas of the 1990s. However, where Carey had the edge is in the song-writing department – on *Music Box*, all but one of the ten tracks bears her name. She was also, in the early 1990s at least, clearly savvy at picking the right collaborators, including a host of big-name producers.

**Number One singles:**
US: Dreamlover; Hero
UK: Without You

**Grammy awards:** None

**Label:**
US: Columbia; UK: CBS

**Recorded in:**
Various locations, USA

**Personnel:**
Mariah Carey
Michael Landau
Walter Afanasieff
Dave Hall
Babyface
David Cole
Kayo
Robert Clivilles
Ren Klyce

**Producers:**
Mariah Carey
Walter Afanasieff
Dave Hall
Babyface
Daryl Simmons
Robert Clivilles

1 Dreamlover (3:54)
2 Hero (4:20)
3 Anytime You Need A Friend (4:26)
4 Music Box (4:58)
5 Now That I Know (4:19)
6 Never Forget You (3:47)
7 Without You (3:36)
8 Just To Hold You Once Again (3:59)
9 I've Been Thinking About You (4:48)
10 All I've Ever Wanted (3:52)

Total album length: 51 minutes

# 22 Let's Talk About Love

| **• Album sales:** 11,800,000 | **• Release date:** November 1997 |

Having established herself as a major player with the previous year's *Falling Into You*, Dion's follow-up was tailor-made to maintain her position. Duets with Barbara Streisand, Luciano Pavarotti, the Bee Gees and Carole King helped create a strong album, yet Dion's stirring, powerful vocal delivery ensure that she is never overshadowed by her accomplices.

The theme song to fellow-Canadian James Cameron's 1997 Oscar-winning movie *Titanic* – the James Horner/Will Jennings composed 'My Heart Will Go On' – is there for those who didn't buy the single or the movie soundtrack. Cuts of lower profile, such as Carole Bayer Sager's 'When I Need You', once a smash for Leo Sayer, stick in the mind and provide radio-friendly fodder.

**Number One singles:** US & UK: My Heart Will Go On

**Grammy awards:** Record of the year; Song of the year; Best female pop vocal performance; Best song written for a motion picture or for television.

**Label:** US: 550 Music
UK: Epic

**Recorded in:**
Various locations, USA

**Personnel:**
Celine Dion
Barbra Streisand
Maurice Gibb (d.2003)
Barry Gibb
Robin Gibb
Diana King
Luciano Pavarotti
Carole King
Michael Landau
Peter Zizzo
Dann Huff
Dean Parks
Walter Afanasieff
Dan Shea
David Foster
Corey Hart
Pino Palladino
Nathan East
Kenny Aronoff
Vinnie Colaiuta
Mike Baird
Bashiri Johnson
Raphael Padilla
Paulinho Da Costa
Steve Porcaro

**Producers:**
David Foster
George Martin
Walter Afanasieff
Corey Hart
Luciano Pavarotti

1 The Reason (5:01)
2 Immortality (4:11))
3 Treat Her Like A Lady (4:05)
4 Why Oh Why (4:50)
5 Love Is On The Way (4:25)
6 Tell Him (4:51)
7 Where Is the Love (4:55)
8 When I Need You (4:12)
9 Miles To Go (Before I Sleep) (4:40)
10 Us (5:47)
11 Just A Little Bit of Love (4:06)
12 My Heart Will Go On (Love Theme From *Titanic*) (4:40)
13 I Hate You Then I Love You (4:43)
14 To Love You More (5:28)
15 Let's Talk About Love (5:12)

Total album length: 71 minutes

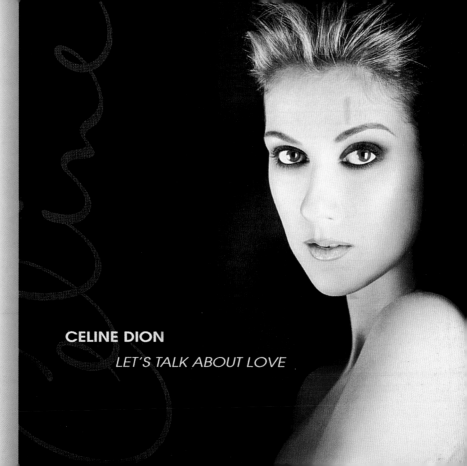

**CELINE DION**

*LET'S TALK ABOUT LOVE*

# 21 Titanic

| • **Album sales:** 11,900,000 | • **Release date:** November 1997 |

Along with lyricist Will Jennings, orchestral composer James Horner landed himself an Oscar for the love theme from *Titanic*, the Celine Dion-sung 'My Heart Will Go On'. Horner won yet another Academy Award for the overall score he wrote for the blockbuster movie.

Although Dion's monster worldwide hit would certainly have boosted sales of this original soundtrack album, Horner's haunting score, ranging from the majestic to the intricately delicate, was sought after in its own right by the movie's legions of fans worldwide.

A former student of the London College of Music, Los Angeles-born Horner started his composing career scoring Roger Corman B-movies. By the early 1980s he entered the big studio network, working on *48 Hours* and *Star Trek II*, amongst others. By the 1990s he was at the top of his game working on blockbuster after blockbuster, receiving Oscar nominations for *Braveheart* and *Apollo 13*.

By the time *Titanic* came along Horner's epic sweep – avoiding excessive sentiment or grandiloquence – was his trademark.

**Number One singles:**
US & UK: My Heart Will Go On

**Grammys:** Record of the year; Song of the year; Best song written for a motion picture or television

**Label:** US & UK: Sony Classics

**Recorded in:**
Los Angeles, USA

**Personnel:**
Sissel
Celine Dion
Simon Franglen
Tony Hinnigan
James Horner
Randy Kerber
Ian Underwood

**Producer:**
James Horner

1 Never an Absolution (3:03)
2 Distant Memories (2:24)
3 Southampton (4:020)
4 Rose (2:52)
5 Leaving Port (3:26)
6 'Take Her To Sea, Mr. Murdoch' (4:31)
7 'Hard To Starboard' (6:52)
8 Unable To Stay, Unwilling To Leave (3:57)
9 The Sinking (5:05)
10 Death Of Titanic (8:26)
11 A Promise Kept (6:03)
12 A Life So Changed (2:13)
13 An Ocean Of Memories (7:58)
14 My Heart Will Go On (Love Theme from *Titanic*) (5:11)
15 Hymn To The Sea (6:26)

Total album length: 123 minutes

MUSIC FROM THE MOTION PICTURE

# TITANIC

MUSIC COMPOSED AND CONDUCTED BY JAMES HORNER

# 20 II

| • Album sales: 12,000,000 | • Release date: August 1994 |

When the first single from an album shoots to the top of the charts in the US, only to be replaced two months later by the follow-up, the album has definitely hit the big time. This was what happened with Boyz II Men's second album, simply titled *II,* and the tracks 'I'll Make Love To You' and 'On Bended Knee'.

If ever a second album consolidated a band's reputation, this was it. Shawn Stockman, Michael McCary and Nathan and Wanya Morris infuse their album with R&B and soul flavours. Working with some of the hottest talent around, including Babyface, Jimmy Jam and Terry Lewis, the band turned out an album that both played to the dance floor and showed off the Philadelphia quartet's stunning vocal interplay.

Generally the slower numbers showed best the band's penchant for technically impressive vocal gymnastics, of which they had become pre-eminent exponents. Their vocal prowess is displayed to most stunning effect on the closing track – an audacious a capella rendition of John Lennon and Paul McCartney's 'Yesterday'.

**Number One singles:**
US: I'll Make Love To You;
On Bended Knee

**Grammy awards:** Best
R&B album; Best R&B
performance by a duo or
group with vocals

**Label:** US: Motown
UK: Dts

**Recorded in:**
Various locations

**Personnel:**
Shawn Stockman
Michael S McCary
Nathan Morris
Wanya Morris

**Producers:**
Dallas Austin
Jimmy Jam
Babyface
Terry Lewis
L A Reid
Tony Rich

1 Thank You (4:34)
2 All Around The World (4:56)
3 U Know (4:46)
4 Vibin' (4:27)
5 I Sit Away (4:34)
6 Jezebel (6:06)
7 Khalil (Interlude) (1:41)
8 Trying Times (5:23)
9 I'll Make Love To You (4:07)
10 On Bended Knee (5:29)
11 50 Candles (5:06)
12 Water Runs Dry (3:21)
13 Yesterday (3:07)

Total album length: 58 minutes

**Boyz II Men**

# 19 Yourself Or Someone Like You

| • **Album sales:** 12,000,000 | • **Release date:** October 1996 |

Influences as wide as Pearl Jam, REM, Tom Petty, early Van Morrison – even a hint of the Velvet Underground – are among the sources that inform this impressive alternative rock debut. In the wake of the Seattle grunge outbreak, Matchbox 20's writer and singer Rob Thomas continued to fly the flag, while sticking within the parameters of mainstream album rock.

Favouring the solid workmanlike approach, Thomas delivers a clutch of confident, well-crafted frill-free songs all benefiting from his sturdy delivery. *Yourself Or Someone Like You* falls into the category of an all-time classic US rock album, standing proud in its own terms, but harking back to halcyon moments in modern American music's rich heritage.

Content-wise, the Georgia foursome tackle a trawl through contemporary Americana taking in troubled love, unrealized dreams and urban confusion. Monosyllabic titles, like 'Push', 'Damn' and 'Argue', emphasise the no-mess approach.

Initially dismissed by some as a flash in the pan, Matchbox 20 proved their critics wrong and stayed the distance. *Yourself Or Someone Like You* may have never topped the charts, but it sold and sold. Within two years it was five times platinum and by 2000 it had doubled that.

| **Number One singles:** | **Personnel:** |
|---|---|
| None | Rob Thomas |
| | Kyle Cook |
| **Grammy awards:** None | Adam Gaynor |
| | Brian Yale |
| **Label:** US & UK: Lava - Atlantic | Paul Doucette |
| | **Producers:** |
| **Recorded in:** Atlanta, USA | Matt Serletic |

1 **Real World** (3:50)
2 **Long Day** (3:45)
3 **3 A M** (3:46)
4 **Push** (3:59)
5 **Girl Like That** (3:45)
6 **Back 2 Good** (5:40)
7 **Damn** (3:20)
8 **Argue** (2:58)
9 **Kody** (4:03)
10 **Busted** (4:15)
11 **Shame** (3:35)

Total album length: 46 minutes

# matchbox 20

*yourself or someone like you*

# 18 Ten

| • Album sales: 12,100,000 | • Release date: August 1991 |

Pearl Jam's debut album, *Ten,* was released just one month before Nirvana's *Nevermind*. Although the Pearl Jam album didn't catch as big a wave initially, it stayed around longer and eventually outsold Nirvana in the US. Guitarist Stone Gossard and bassist Jeff Ament who, together with singer Eddie Vedder, wrote most of the album, had paid their dues in metal rock bands, and the influence shows. Of all the groups that forged the Seattle grunge sound, it was Pearl Jam that made it most accessible, purveying a radio friendliness that didn't alienate fans of more traditional rock forms.

It was vocalist Vedder, with his gravelly baritone and tortured, passionate delivery, who was pivotal in identifying Pearl Jam with the Seattle sound.

Ament and Gossard had been in an earlier band, Mother Love Bone, but in 1990 its singer, Andrew Wood, died from a heroin overdose. When they then teamed up with Vedder their first choice for a band name was Mookie Blaylock, after the NBA basketball star. The group changed the name to Pearl Jam before their debut effort was released. However, the album title, *Ten*, is taken from the number on Mookie Blaylock's vest.

**Number One singles:**
None

**Grammy awards:**
None

**Label**: US & UK: Epic

**Recorded in:**
Seattle, USA

**Personnel:**
Eddie Vedder
Mike McCreedy
Stone Gossard
Jeff Ament
Dave Krusen
Walter Gray
Rick Parashar
Tim Palmer

**Producers:**
Rick Parashar
Pearl Jam

1  Once (3:51)
2  Even Flow (4:53)
3  Alive (5:40)
4  Why Go (3:19)
5  Black (5:48)
6  Jeremy (5:18)
7  Oceans (2:41)
8  Porch (3:30)
9  Garden (4:58)
10 Deep (4:18)
11 Release (6:30)

Total album length: 51 minutes

**Pearl Jam**

PEARL JAM

# 17 Breathless

| • Album sales: 12,100,000 | • Release date: October 1992 |

Kenny G's light and breezy style has won him the considerable accolade of the best-selling saxophonist of all time and *Breathless* is one of his best-selling albums.

Having risen to prominence in the 1980s, by the 1990s Kenny G was a global artist much favoured by middle-of-the-road and easy-listening radio stations. Although derided by jazz purists, his fluid phrasing and mellow style earned him an army of fans. Criticism from the jazz cognoscenti was of no matter to Kenny G who, by his own admission, was simply a pop instrumentalist, and a very popular one at that.

The former horn man for Barry White's Love Unlimited Orchestra certainly delivers some great, feelgood pop cuts on *Breathless*, ranging from 'The Joy of Life' to 'End Of The Night' and 'Forever In Love'. Legendary rhythm and blues singer Aaron Neville adds to the celebration with a welcome vocal on 'Even If My Heart Would Break'. Peabo Bryson adds vocal colour on the soulful 'By The Time The Night Is Over'.

**Numer One singles:** None

**Grammy awardss:**
Best Instrumental Composition

**Label:** US & UK: Arista

**Recorded in:**
Seattle, Sausalito, & Los Angeles, USA

**Personnel:**
Kenny G
Peabo Bryson
Aaron Neville
Dean Parks
Michael Thompson
Walter Afanasieff
Dan Shea
Vail Johnson
John Robinson
Paulinho Da Costa

**Producers:**
Kenny G
Walter Afanasieff
David Foster
Dan Shea

1 The Joy Of Life (4:19)
2 Forever In Love (4:58)
3 In The Rain (4:59)
4 Sentimental (6:34)
5 By The Time This Night Is Over (4:45)
6 End Of The Night (5:21)
7 Alone (5:24)
8 Morning (5:13)
9 Even If My Heart Would Break (4:58))
10 G Bop (4:05)
11 Sister Rose (6:13)
12 A Year Ago (5:15)
13 Homeland (4:32)
14 The Wedding Song (3:21)

Total album length: 70 minutes

KENNY G
BREATHLESS

# 16 Forrest Gump

| **Album sales:** 12,100,000 | **Release date:** August 1994 |

This selection of popular music from the 1950s, 1960s and 1970s – collected together for the *Forrest Gump* soundtrack – was a powerful one. Many of the most significant artists of the preceding decades were included, from Aretha Franklin to The Doors, usually performing a strong song from their repertoire.

While any well-compiled collection of classics stands a good chance of chart success, this had the advantage of accompanying one of the most popular films of the 1990s. Despite attracting some criticism at the time for its reactionary political stance, the Tom-Hanks-starring *Forrest Gump*, the tale of a simpleton's journey through some of America's recent historical milestones, proved a massive box office smash and won the Oscar for Best Picture in 1995.

| | |
|---|---|
| **Number One singles:** None | **Recorded in:** Various locations |
| **Grammy awards:** None | **Personnel:** Various artists |
| **Label:** US & UK: Epic | **Producers:** Various producers |

1 Hound Dog (Elvis Presley) (2:16)
2 Rebel Rouser (Duane Eddy) (2:22)
3 But I Do (Henry, Clarence 'Frogman') (2:18)
4 Walk Right In (The Rooftop Singers) (2:33)
5 Land Of 1000 Dances (Wilson Pickett) (2:25)
6 Blowin' In The Wind (Joan Baez) (2:36)
7 Fortunate Son (Creedence Clearwater Revival) (2:18)
8 I Can't Help Myself (The Four Tops) 2:43
9 Respect (Aretha Franklin) (2:27)
10 Rainy Day Women #12 & 35 (Bob Dylan) (4:35)
11 Sloop John B (The Beach Boys) (2:56)
12 California Dreamin' (The Mamas & the Papas) (2:39)
13 For What It's Worth (Buffalo Springfield) (2:38)
14 What The World Needs Now Is Love (Jackie DeShannon) (3:13)
15 Break on Through (The Doors) (2:27)
16 Mrs Robinson (Simon & Garfunkel) (3:51)
17 Volunteers (Jefferson Airplane) (2:04)
18 Let's Get Together (The Youngbloods) 4:36

19 San Francisco (Scott McKenzie) (2:58)
20 Turn! Turn! Turn! (The Byrds) (3:54)
21 Aquarius/Let The Sunshine In (The Fifth Dimension) (4:48)
22 Everybody's Talkin' (Harry Nilsson) (2:44)
23 Joy To The World (Three Dog Night) (3:16)
24 Stoned Love (The Supremes) (2:59)
25 Raindrops Keep Falling On My Head (BJ Thomas) (3:00)
26 Mr. President (Randy Newman) (2:46)
27 Sweet Home Alabama (Lynyrd Skynyrd) (4:43)
28 Running on Empty (Jackson Browne) (4:56)
29 It Keeps You Runnin' (The Doobie Brothers) (4:13)
30 I've Got To Use My Imagination (Gladys Knight & the Pips) (3:30)
31 Go Your Own Way (Fleetwood Mac) (3:39)
32 On The Road Again Willie Nelson) (2:29)
33 Against The Wind (Bob Seger) (5:53)
34 Forrest Gump Suite (Alan Silvestri) (8:49)

Total album length: 114 minutes

34 AMERICAN CLASSICS ON 2 CDs

# Forrest Gump
## The Soundtrack

SPECIAL COLLECTORS' EDITION

# 15 Wide Open Spaces

| • **Album sales:** 12,100,000 | • **Release date:** January 1998 |

Sweet harmonies, exemplary acoustic country playing and deft, understated arrangements have always distinguished albums from the Dixie Chicks. By the time *Wide Open Spaces* came along, the founding sisters, Martie Seidel and Emily Erwin, had been performing together for almost a decade. They were joined and somewhat rejuvenated by the arrival of Natalie Maines on lead vocal duties.

The support of a major label, Monument, may have helped draw in a larger audience, but the scintillating three-way vocal interplay, sensitively backed by guitar, fiddle and banjo was enough to command a healthy following its own right to.

The powerful performances are supported by a beguiling blend of defiant mid-tempo rockers and sad, wistful ballads. The album closes with contributions from female writers: Maria McKee's 'Am I The Only One (Who's Ever Felt This Way)' and 'Give It Up Or Let Me Go' by Bonnie Raitt.

**Number One singles:**
None

**Grammy awards:** Best country album; Best country performance by a duo or group with vocals

**Label:** US: Monument; UK: Epic

**Recorded in:**
Nashville, USA

**Personnel:**
Natalie Maines
Emily Erwin
Martie Seidel
Mark Casstevens
Martie Seidel
Matt Rollings
Lloyd Maines
Tony Paoletta
Natalie Maines
Billy Crain
Billy Joe Walker Jr
Paul Worley
Bobby Charles Jr
Joe Chemay
Michael Rhodes
Tom Roady
Greg Morrows
George Marinelli
Tommy Nash

**Producers:**
Jim Burnett
Mark Cappsr
Tony Castle
Blake Chancey
Erik Hellerman
Clarke Schleicher
Ed Simonton
Paul Worley

1  I Can Love You Better  (3:53)
2  Wide Open Spaces  (3:44)
3  Loving Arms  (3:37)
4  There's Your Trouble  (3:10)
5  You Were Mine  (3:37)
6  Never Say Die  (3:56)
7  Tonight the Heartache's on Me  (3:25)
8  Let 'Er Rip  (2:49)
9  Once You've Loved Somebody  (3:28)
10  I'll Take Care Of You  (3:40)
11  Am I The Only One (Who's Ever Felt This...)  (3:25)
12  Give It Up Or Let Me Go  (4:55)

Total album length: 44 minutes

# 14 The Woman In Me

| • Album sales: 12,300,000 | • Release date: July 1995 |

Shania Twain's newfound romantic and professional partnership with studio-ace 'Mutt' Lange propelled the dimuntive songstress from country darling to global megastar. Lange's production skills had thus far seen him polishing up metal acts such as Def Leppard and AC/DC, making them shine for a mainstream audience. His partnership with Twain found him attempting to take country to a pop audience.

What the writing team of Twain and Lange produces is a sassy combination of witty well-crafted lyrics, strong melodies and hooks, all shown off to best effect by deft arrangements.

Twain's solid yet agile voice is just as at home with the traditional country of 'Who's Bed Have Your Boots Been Under?' as it is with the rockier 'You Win My Love' or the balladry of 'Home Ain't Where His Heart Is (Anymore)'.

Many pop acts have been fashioned by studio svengalis but Twain – with a little help from Lange – is one act who invented herself. *The Woman In Me* is where the big story started.

**Number One singles:**
None

**Grammy awards:**
Best country album

**Label:** US & UK:
Mercury

**Recorded in:**
St Anne des Lacs, Canada;
Nashville, USA

**Producer:**
Robert John 'Mutt' Lange

**Personnel:**
Shania Twain
Larry Byrom
Dann Huff
Brent Rowan
Brent Mason
Billy Crain
John Hughey
Paul Franklin
Paul Franklin
Sam Bush
Ron Hajacos
Joe Spivey
Glen Duncan
Hargus 'Pig' Robbins
David Hungate
Brent Mason
Various other personnel

1  Home Ain't Where His Heart Is (Anymore) (4:12)
2  Any Man Of Mine (4:07)
3  Whose Bed Have Your Boots Been Under? (4:25)
4  (If You're Not In It For Love) I'm Outta... (4:30)
5  The Woman In Me (Needs The Man In You) (4:50)
6  Is There Life After Love? (4:39)
7  If It Don't Take Two (3:40)
8  You Win My Love (4:26)
9  Raining on Our Love (4:38)
10 Leaving Is The Only Way Out (4:07)
11 No One Needs To Know (3:04)
12 God Bless The Child (1:30)

Total album length: 48 minutes

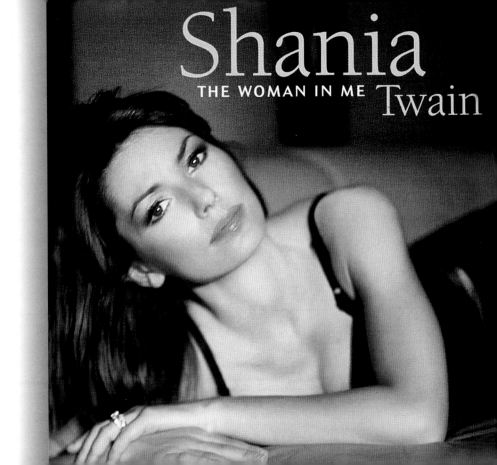

# 13 Falling Into You

| • Album sales: 13,100,000 | • Release date: March 1996 |

French-Canadian chanteuse Celine Dion already had legions of fans from the faithful AOR market when this polished collection of songs burst on to the scene, guaranteeing her a sure-fire winner. For many, the strength of Dion's voice alone is enough, and here it's shown off to dazzling effect across a variety of styles.

Jim Steinman provides Dion with an arresting opener with 'It's All Coming Back to Me Now'.

Elsewhere, she effortlessly tackles powerful ballads like Diane Warren's 'Because You Love Me', the theme song from *Up Close And Personal*. The song won the 1997 Grammy for Best Song Written Specifically for a Motion Picture or Television. The album was also nominated for Record Of The Year, Song Of The Year and Best Female Pop Vocal Performance.

Ike and Tina Turner's 'River Deep, Mountain High' also gets the lavish Dion treatment, as does Eric Carmen's haunting 'All By Myself'.

**Number One singles:** US: Because You Loved Me

**Grammys:** Best pop album; Album of the year

**Label:** US: 550 Music
UK: Epic

**Recorded in:**
Various locations

**Personnel:**
Celine Dion
Gary 'Headman' Hasse
Paul Buckmaster
Aldo Nova
Jeff Smallwood

Ottmar Liebert
Steve Farris
Tim Pierce
Eddie Martinez
Michael Thompson
Andre Coutu
Chris Taylor
Basile Leroux
David Foster
Roy Bittan
Vavious other personnel

**Producers:**
Jim Steinman
David Foster
Rick Nowels
Billy Steinberg
Ric Wake

1 It's All Coming Back To Me Now (7:37)
2 Because You Loved Me (Theme from *Up Close And Personal*) (4:33)
3 Falling Into You (4:18)
4 Make You Happy (4:31)
5 Seduces Me (3:46)
6 All By Myself (5:12)
7 Declaration Of Love (4:20)
8 Dreaming Of You (5:07)
9 I Love You (5:30)
10 If That's What It Takes (4:12)
11 I Don't Know (4:38)
12 River Deep-Mountain High (4:10)
13 Call The Man (6:08)
14 Fly ( 2:58)

Total album length: 68 minutes

FALLING INTO YOU

*Céline*

DION

# 12 Metallica

| • **Album sales:** 13,300,000 | • **Release date:** July 1991 |

Metallica's 1988 album *And Justice for All...* perhaps best exemplified the band's progressive hard metal sound, but for their 1991 follow-up the group decided to explore previously uncharted territory – the mainstream.

An expertly crafted marriage of production and musicianship, *Metallica* (also known as *The Black Album*) was, as its title was intended to suggest, something of a renaissance for a group who had developed an enviable reputation largely without the benefit of airplay. The name was also a signal for listeners to concentrate on the stripped down songs, rather than the packaging. For the first time Metallica recruited the services of an outside producer, Bob Rock, who was brought in on the strength of his work on Motley Crue's *Dr Feelgood* album. Rock's task was to give the new recording a deliberately 'bigger', more listener-friendly sound.

The songs were written during a two-month period in the summer of 1990. However, it would take ten months in the studio – at a cost of around a million dollars – and a certain degree of tension with between producer and band members, before the album was completed. The final product was debuted at a free party in New York's Madison Square Gardens, where it received an enthusiastic response from fans.

**Number One singles:**
None

**Grammy awards:** Best Metal performance with vocal

**Label:** US: Elektra; UK: Phonogram

**Recorded in:**
Los Angeles, USA

**Personnel:**
James Hetfield
Kirk Hammett
Jason Newstead
Lars Ulrich

**Producers:**
Bob Rock
James Hetfield
Lars Ulrich

1  **Enter Sandman** (5:29)
2  **Sad But True** (5:24)
3  **Holier Than Thou** (3:47)
4  **The Unforgiven** (6:26)
5  **Wherever I May Roam** (6:42)
6  **Don't Tread On Me** (3:59)
7  **Through The Never** (4:01)
8  **Nothing Else Matters** (6:29)
9  **Of Wolf And Man** (4:16)
10 **The God That Failed** (5:05)
11 **My Friend Of Misery** (6:47)
12 **The Struggle Within** (3:51)

Total album length: 62 minutes

# 11 Millennium

| • **Album sales:** 13,300,000 | • **Release date:** May 1999 |

It's impossible to look at the album *Millenium* without acknowledging the phenomenal success Stateside of the band's 1997 predecessor, *Backstreet Boys*. Brought together by Swedish svengali and songwriter Max Martin, the Backstreet Boys had been Euro-pop sensations for a couple of years before this US debut – an amalgam of the best of what they had so far achieved – rocketed them to stardom in America. More than 10,000,000 albums later, the *Backstreet Boys* was still in the Top 40 when their follow-up *Millennium* was released.

How could they follow this success? More of the same was the order of the day with the Backstreet Boys sticking to the tried and tested formula that had powered them to global success. Pop harmonies, irresistible dance grooves and some high-quality balladry were more than enough to keep fans happy, as the single 'I Want It that Way' amply demonstrates.

The album was nominated for the 1999 Grammy award for Album of the Year and for Best Pop Vocal Album. 'I Want It that Way' was up for Record of the Year and Song of the Year and 'Show Me the Meaning of Being Lonely' was nominated for the 2000 Grammy award for Best Pop Performance.

**Number One singles:**
None

**Grammy awards:** None

**Label:** US & UK: Jive

**Recorded in:**
Various locations

**Personnel:**
Kevin Richardson
Howard Dorough
Alexander James Mclean
Brian Littrel
Nick Carter

**Producers:**
Kristian Lundin
Max Martin
Rami
Robert John 'Mutt' Lange
Stephen Lipson

1  **Larger than Life**  (3:52)
2  **I Want It that Way**  (3:33)
3  **Show Me the Meaning of Being Lonely**  (3:54)
4  **It's Gotta Be You**  (2:55)
5  **I Need You Tonight**  (4:25)
6  **Don't Want You Back**  (3:25)
7  **Don't Wanna Lose You Now**  (3:54)
8  **The One**  (3:46)
9  **Back to Your Heart**  (4:21)
10 **Spanish Eyes**  (3:53)
11 **No One Else Comes Close**  (3:42)

Total album length: 46 minutes

# 10 Baby One More Time

| **Album sales:** 13,900,000 | **Release date:** January 1999 |

Britney Spears has Mickey Mouse partly to thank for her rise to stardom; her first spell in the limelight was on the Disney's *New Mickey Mouse Club*. This exposure paved the way for her debut album, *Baby One More Time,* which established Spears as a top teen-pop singer in the tradition of Debbie Gibson and Tiffany.

Already a mature adolescent, Spears peddled her nouveau bubblegum pop with confidence and style, blending the traditional with occasional modern rap and dance inflections. Euro-producer Max Martin, a guiding force behind the Backstreet Boys, made sure Spears had her share of hooky choruses and persuasive melodies, as featured in the title track, and the other hits 'Sometimes' and '(You Drive Me) Crazy'.

Her ambiguous image – part female teenage role model, part coquettish tease – was reflected by her performance in school uniform on the video for the title track. During much of the 1990s teen pop had been eclipsed by more sassy streetwise sounds but, with Britney Spears, bubblegum was back with a vengeance.

**Number One singles:** US & UK: Baby One More Time; UK: Born to Make You Happy

**Grammy awards:** None

**Label:** US & UK: Jive

**Recorded in:** Stockholm, Sweden; New York, USA

**Personnel:**
Britney Spears
Mickie Bassie
Don Philip
Esbjorn Ohrwall
Dan Petty
Eric Foster White
Johan Carlberg
Andrew McIntyre
Max Martin
Per Magnusson
David Kreuger
Kristian Lundin
Doug Petty
Tomas Lindberg
Various other personnel

**Producers:**
Eric Foster White
Kristian Lundian
Per Magnusson
David Kreuger
Max Martin

1 Baby One More Time (3:30)
2 (You Drive Me) Crazy (3:17)
3 Sometimes (4:05)
4 Soda Pop (3:20)
5 Born To Make You Happy (4:03)
6 From The Bottom Of My Broken Heart (5:11)
7 I Will Be There (3:53)
8 I Will Still Love You (4:02)
9 Thinkin' About You (3:35)
10 E-Mail My Heart (3:41)
11 The Beat Goes On (3:40)

Total album length: 42 minutes

Britney Spears

...baby one more time

# 9 Ropin' The Wind

**• Album sales:** 14,000,000 **• Release date:** September 1991

Garth Brooks was an great admirer of Billy Joel. The inclusion of one of Joel's songs, 'Shameless', on *Ropin' The Wind* illuminates the links between the two artists' brand of blue collar balladry, as well as illustrating Brooks' easy ability to straddle the country-pop divide.

The country star's comfort with rock forms is evident throughout the album, from the grand sweep of 'The River', to the honky-tonk excitement of 'The Rodeo' or the epic storytelling of 'In Lonesome Dove'. However, Brooks' strength is that he never turns his back on country – *Ropin' The Wind* attracted hordes of new admirers without ever disenfranchising his country audience. The result speaks for itself: it was the first country album to enter at the top spot of the Billboard Top 200.

Even with the crossover factor, the subject matter remains unswervingly country, as Brooks journeys effortlessly through a world of truckers, jail, drinking, family, love and the Western mythology. Brooks' second album *No Fences* was the release that had broken him into the mainstream. This follow-up established him as an enduring force in popular music.

**Number One singles:**
None

**Grammy awards:** None

**Label:** US & UK: Capitol

**Recorded in:**
Nashville, Tennessee

**Personnel:**
Garth Brooks
Mark Casstevens
Chris Leuzinger
Bruce Bouton

Jerry Douglas
Sam Bush
Rob Hajacos
Bobby Wood
Edgar Meyer
Mike Chapman
Milton Sledge
Trisha Yearwood
Carl Jackson
Larry Cordle
Susan Ashton

**Producer:**
Allen Reynolds

1  **Against The Grain** (2:22)
2  **Rodeo** (3:53)
3  **What She's Doing Now** (3:26)
4  **Burning Bridges** (3:34)
5  **Papa Loved Mama** (4:48)
6  **Shameless** (2:51)
7  **Cold Shoulder** (4:20)
8  **We Bury the Hatchet** (3:55)
9  **In Lonesome Dove** (3:05)
10 **The River** (4:28)

Total album length: 36 minutes

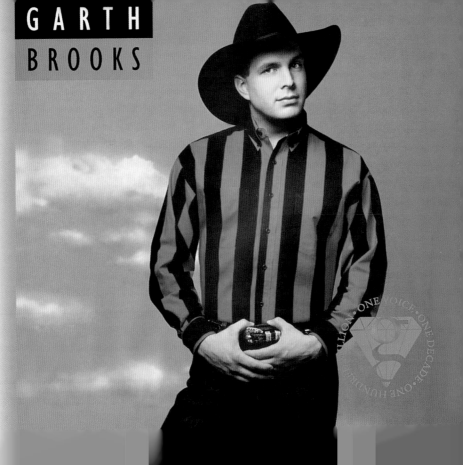

GARTH
BROOKS

# 8 Backstreet Boys

| **Album sales:** 14,100,000 | **Release date:** December 1997 |

Although they formed in Orlando, Florida, it was in Europe – Germany to be precise – that the Backstreet Boys had their first taste of the big time. As a result, it was almost a year later that their eponymous US debut album, a collection of tracks taken from their two European offerings, was released. The delay certainly did them no harm, as it became the third best-selling album of 1998. By then, with the charts peppered with frothy pop from the likes of The Spice Girls and a host of easy listening boy bands, the group slotted neatly into the prevailing scene.

Like their other boy-band contemporaries, the Backstreet Boys served up a menu of fashionably crafted tunes embracing the full gamut from lively dance numbers to languorous ballads and garnished with a spot of rapping and some *a la mode* hip-hop splashes. Despite the hint of menace in their name, the Backstreet Boys were parent-friendly and made music for teenagers to swoon to.

'Get Down (You're The One For Me)', the track that got them started in Europe, was joined on *Backstreet Boys* by a host of radio-friendly smash hits that had already proved their worth on the other side of the Atlantic.

**Number One singles:**
None

**Grammy awards:**
None

**Label:** US & UK: Jive

**Recorded in:** Stockholm, Sweden; Orlando & New York, USA

**Personnel:**
Nick Carter
Brian 'B-Rok' Littrell
Kevin Richardson
Howard Dorough
Alexander James McLean

**Producers:**
Bulent Aris
Denniz Pop
Larry 'Rock' Campbell
Max Martin
Mookie
P M Dawn
Robert John 'Mutt' Lange
Toni Cottura
Veit Renn

1 We've Got It Goin' On (3:39)
2 Quit Playing Games (With My Heart) (3:52)
3 As Long As You Love Me (3:40)
4 Everybody (Backstreet's Back) (4:38)
5 All I Have To Give (4:36)
6 Anywhere For You (4:40)
7 Hey, Mr DJ (Keep Playin' This Song) (4:42)
8 I'll Never Break Your Heart (4:48)
9 Darlin' (5:31)
10 Get Down (You're The One For Me) (3:50)
11 Set Adrift On Memory Bliss (3:30)
12 If You Want It To Be Good Girl (4:49)

Total album length: 49 minutes

# 7 Supernatural

| • Album sales: 14,600,000 | • Release date: June 1999 |

A highly respected guitarist since the 1960s with a supple latin/jazz style, Carlos Santana's career continued to flourish in the 1990s, although mainly on stage. *Supernatural*, his debut album for Arista, marked a successful return to the chart mainstream.

**Number One singles:**
US: Smooth; Maria Maria

**Grammy awards:**
Record of the year; Album of the year; best rock album; best rock performance by a duo or group with vocal; Best pop performance by a duo or group with vocal; Best pop collaboration with vocals; Best rock instrumental performance; Best pop instrumental performance

**Label:** US & UK: Arista

**Recorded in:**
Various locations, USA

**Personnel:**
Carlos Santana
Dave Matthews
Lauryn Hill
Fher
Eagle Eye Cherry
Eric Clapton
Francis Dunnery
Al Anderson
Sergio Vallin
J B Eckl
Danny Wolinski
Mic Gillette
Jose Abel Figueroa
Various other personnel

**Producers include:**
Carlos Santana
Steve Harris
Wyclef Jean
Jerry 'Wonder' Duplessis
K C Porter

Santana's reputation secured the participation of performers as diverse as the Eric Clapton, the Dust Brothers, Everlast, Lauryn Hill and Eagle-Eye Cherry. The result was an eclectic mix of styles and genres, underlined by Santana's Latin roots and scintillating guitar work.

The album reached Number One in 23 countries and gave Santana two US Number One singles, 'Maria Maria' and 'Smooth' (which reached Number Six and Number 75, respectively, in the UK). Santana also swept the board at that year's Grammys, winning three awards for *Supernatural* as an album and another five for individual songs from it.

1 (Da Le) Yalleo (5:51)
2 Love Of My Life (5:48)
3 Put Your Lights On (4:47)
4 Africa Bamba (4:40)
5 Smooth (4:56)
6 Do You Like The Way (5:52)
7 Maria, Maria (4:21)
8 Migra (5:24)
9 Corazon Espinado (4:32)
10 Wishing It Was (4:59)
11 El Farol (4:49)
12 Primavera (5:17)
13 The Calling (7:48)

Total album length: 69 minutes

SUPERNATURAL

Santana

# 6 Double Live

| • Album sales: 15,000,000 | • Release date: November 1998 |

1990s country phenomenon Garth Brooks was ten albums into his career before his first live album was released. To keep his fans happy, each of the 25 cuts on the album was recorded at a different gig, ensuring that the souvenir hunters would be first in line.

The albums does not disappoint, delivering crisp renditions of all Brooks' favourites. Although he stays pretty faithful to the studio originals, the audience does get a look-in on many tracks, notably 'Unanswered Prayers', 'The Dance', 'Shameless' and 'That Summer', all of which are lifted above their original versions by audience participation. Those who want something more than a 'best of' package are not disappointed, either. Not only does he add extra verses to 'Friends in Low Places' and 'The Thunder Rolls', there are also three previously unreleased numbers, including 'It's Your Song', 'Wild As The Wind,' and 'Tearin' It Up (and Burnin' It Down)'.

**Number One singles:**
None

**Grammy awards:** None

**Label:** US & UK: Capitol

**Recorded in:**
Various locations, USA

**Personnel:**
Garth Brooks
Trisha Yearwood
Charles Cochran
Jimmy Mattingly
Debbie Nims

Steve Wariner
Stephanie Davis
Mark Casstevens
Ty England
James Garver
Steve McClure
Chris Leuzinger
Gordon Kennedy
John Kinsch
Keith Urban
Bruce Bouton
Various other personnel

**Producers:**
Allen Reynolds
Carlton Davis

1 Callin' Baton Rouge (2:58)
2 Two of A Kind, Workin' On A Full House (2:44)
3 Shameless (3:55)
4 Papa Loved Mama (2:51)
5 The Thunder Rolls (4:48)
6 We Shall Be Free (4:43)
7 Unanswered Prayers (3:41)
8 Standing Outside The Fire (3:43)
9 Longneck Bottle (2:42)
10 It's Your Song (4:18)
11 Much Too Young (To Feel This Damn Old) (3:12)
12 The River (3:48)
13 Tearin' It Up (And Burnin' It Down) (3:56)
14 Ain't Goin' Down ('Til The Sun Comes Up) (4:45)
15 Rodeo (3:44)
16 The Beaches Of Cheyenne (3:51)
17 Two Pina Coladas (4:38)
18 Wild As The Wind (4:10)
19 To Make You Feel My Love (3:17)
20 That Summer (4:42)
21 American Honky-Tonk Bar Association (4:05)
22 If Tomorrow Never Comes (3:44)
23 The Fever (3:40)
24 Friends In Low Places (8:56)
25 The Dance (3:56)

Total album length: 101 minutes

DOUBLE LIVE    **g**    ARTH BROOKS

2 CD SET

# 5 No Fences

| • Album sales: 16,000,000 | • Release date: August 1990 |

Seen by many as the saviour of country music, Garth Brooks took traditional country idioms and reinterpreted them using pop hooks and rock-n'-roll attitude. His second major release, *No Fences*, saw him grow more confident in his role as the aspirant new king of country. As with his female counterpart, Shania Twain, his success relied a his skilful blend of old and the new, creating music that would appeal to listeners across a wide spectrum.

Brooks is in particularly fine form on the album's ballads, where soft folk tones and tougher rock arrangements are used to striking effect. His blue-collar credentials are carefully maintained on the likes of the honky-tonk-ish 'Friends In Low Places', one of the album's five hit singles. The other three singles, 'The Thunder Rolls', 'Two Of A Kind', 'Workin' On A Full House' and 'Unanswered Prayers', helped extend the album's shelf life and notch up impressive sales.

*No Fences* as a whole is of a consistent high quality, with the moving 'New Way To Fly' and the infectious 'Mr Blue' showing him at ease with both heartbreak and humour. With cowboy hat already in place, *No Fences* set the standard by which Brooks meant to continue.

**Number One singles:**
None

**Grammy awards:** None

**Label:** US & UK: Capitol

**Recorded in:**
Nashville, USA

**Personnel:**
Garth Brooks
Chris Leuzinger
Pat Alger
Johnny Christopher
Mark Casstevens
Bruce Bouton
Rob Hajacos
Bobby Wood
Edgar Meyer
Milton Sledge
Mike Chapman

**Producer:**
Allen Reynolds

1 **The Thunder Rolls** (3:42)
2 **New Way To Fly** (3:54)
3 **Two Of A Kind, Workin' On A Full House** (2:31)
4 **Victim Of The Game** (2:17)
5 **Friends In Low Places** (4:18)
6 **Wild Horses** (3:08)
7 **Unanswered Prayers** (3:23)
8 **Same Old Story** (2:52)
9 **Mr Blue** (3:16)
10 **Wolves** (4:08)

Total album length: 33 minutes

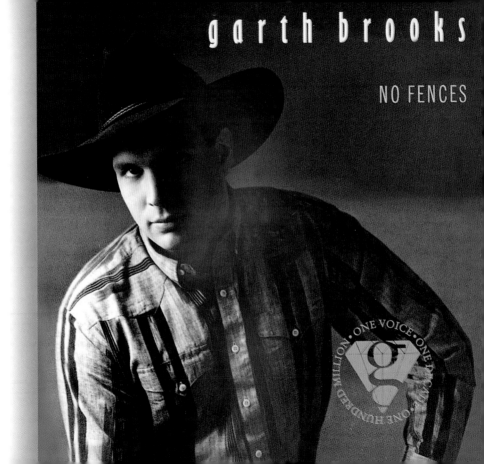

# 4 Cracked Rear View

| • **Album sales:** 16,100,000 | • **Release date:** December 1994 |

To sell more than 16 million copies of your first major album (an earlier indie release, *Koochypop*, had come out in 1993) is no mean feat, but that was exactly what Hootie & the Blowfish managed with *Cracked Rear View*. It certainly helped that the album was an extremely confident and mature entré, packed to the rafters with harmonies and hooks. Clearly their early years as a standard rock covers band had honed their skills and allowed them to develop the songwriting skills which bloomed here with a host of tunes penned by the band.

Hootie and Co were hardly charting new or unmapped territory, they simply delivered up straight-down-the-line, soft-to-firm rock in an extremely palatable form. Tracks like 'Hold My Hand' and 'Let Her Cry', which earned them a Best Pop Performance Grammy, bear an easy rock hallmark similar to predecessors as diverse as the Allman Brothers and REM.

Completing the picture is the distinctive baritone vocal style of Darius Rucker whose delivery lends an authority to Hootie & the Blowfish material that may have been lacking with a weaker singer. This may have been their major-label debut, but the band found the right formula and stuck to it.

**Number One singles:**
None

**Grammy awards:** Best new artist; Best pop performance by a duo or group with vocal

**Label:** US & UK: Atlantic

**Recorded in:**
North Hollywood, USA

**Personnel:**
Mark Bryan
Darius Rucker
Dean Felber
Jim 'Soni' Sonefeld

**Producers:**
Don Gehman

1  Hannah Jane (3:33)
2  Hold My Hand (4:15)
3  Let Her Cry (5:08)
4  Only Wanna Be With You (3:46)
5  Running From An Angel (3:37)
6  I'm Goin' Home (4:10)
7  Drowning (5:01)
8  Time (4:53)
9  Look Away (2:38)
10 Not Even The Trees (4:37)
11 Goodbye (4:05)
12 Untitled (3:33)

Total album length: 43 minutes

# HOOTIE & THE BLOWFISH

*cracked rear view*

# 3 Jagged Little Pill

| • **Album sales:** 19,000,000 | • **Release date:** June 1995 |

Rarely has 'angry' been so popular as on this angst-ridden Alanis Morissette album. Hell hath no fury like a woman scorned is writ large as the mantra for this collection of embittered love songs, sung, yelled and shouted by the 19-year-old Canadian. Her painful encounters with love, and their public exorcism, struck a chord and in the process redirected the singer from campus leftfield to full-on mainstream.

Fortunately for Morissette, her bitter pill was made more palatable by a saccharine gloss provided by the pop sensibilities of her musical collaborator Glen Ballard, with whom she co-wrote the album. Yet it was her in-your-face rants that engaged listeners and landed her two Grammy awards. A combination of traditional techniques such as power chords and acoustic guitar embellishments, combined with of-the-moment touches, created a soundscape that seemed both familiar and immediate.

Although she had enjoyed a couple of releases in Canada before *Jagged Little Pill*, this was her first proper release in the US and the rest of the world – and what an entrance it was!

**Number One singles:**
None

**Grammy awards:** Album of the year; Best rock album; Best rock song – You Oughta Know; Best female rock vocal performance – You Oughta Know

**Label:** US & UK: Maverick

**Recorded in:** Hollywood, USA

**Personnel:**
Alanis Morissette
Glen Ballard
Basil Fung
Joel Shearer
Michael Landau
Dave Navarro
Benmont Tench
Lance Morrison
Flea
Rob Ladd
Matt Laug
Gota Yashiki

**Producer:**
Glen Ballard

1 All I Really Want (4:44)
2 You Oughta Know (4:09)
3 Perfect (3:07)
4 Hand In My Pocket (3:41)
5 Right Through You (2:55)
6 Forgiven (5:00)
7 You Learn (3:59)
8 Head Over Feet (4:27)
9 Mary Jane (4:40)
10 Ironic (3:49)
11 Not The Doctor (3:47)
12 Wake Up (4:53)
13 You Oughta Know (8:12)

Total album length: 54 minutes

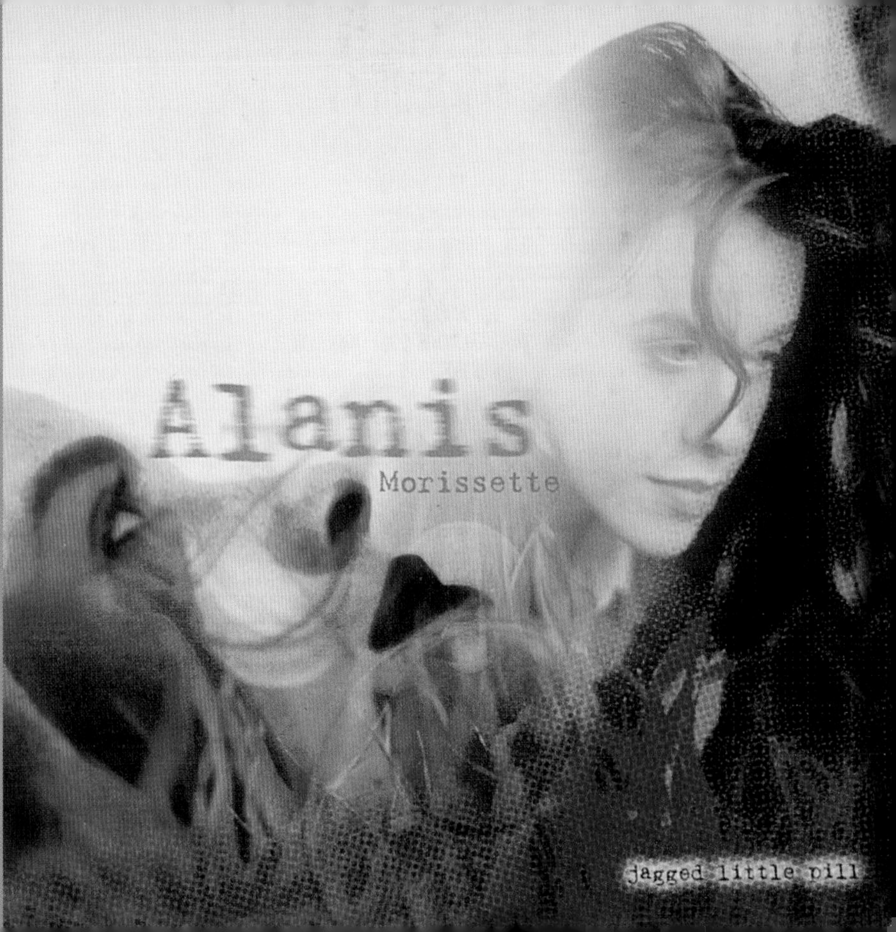
Alanis
Morissette
jagged little pill

# 2 The Bodyguard

| **Album sales:** 19,100,000 | **Release date:** November 1992 |

Country chanteuse Dolly Parton is probably as much responsible for the success of this collection as is Whitney Houston herself. It was Parton who penned the intense ballad which would propel *The Bodyguard* into the record books. 'I Will Always Love You' gave Houston the room to emote massively, helping secure the song an astonishing 14-week run at the top of the Billboard singles chart.

This is one of those rare examples where the music from a film – assisted by Houston's performance of it – outshines the movie and propels the film to greater heights than it might have enjoyed otherwise. *The Bodyguard* was by no means a one song album. Houston provided another seven tracks, including 'Run To You' and 'I'm Every Woman', and other artists including Kenny G, Joe Cocker, and Aaron Neville also contribute. A stand-out track, in an album comprised of strong writing and performances is Curtis Stigers' rendition of Nick Lowe's 'Peace, Love and Understanding'.

**Number One singles:**
US & UK: I Will Always Love You

**Grammy awards:**
Album of the Year

**Label:** US & UK: Arista

**Recorded in:**
Various locations

**Personnel:**
Whitney Houston
Aaron Neville
Curtis Stigers

Joe Cocker
Kenny G
LIsa Stansfield
Curtis Stiger
Various other personnel

**Producers:**
Narada Michael Walden
L A Reid
Ian Devaney
Jazz Summers
Clive Davis
BeBe Winans
Babyface
Various other producers

1 I Will Always Love You  (Whitney Houston)  (4:31)
2 I Have Nothing  (Whitney Houston)  (4:48)
3 I'm Every Woman  (Whitney Houston)  (4:45)
4 Run To You  (Whitney Houston)  (4:22)
5 Queen Of The Night  (Whitney Houston)  (3:08)
6 Jesus Loves Me  (Whitney Houston)  (5:11)
7 Even If My Heart Would Break  (Aaron Neville)  (4:58)
8 Someday (I'm Coming Back)  (Lisa Stansfield)  (4:57)
9 It's Gonna Be A Lovely Day  (S.O.U.L. S.Y.S.T.E.M.)  (4:47)
10 (What's So Funny 'Bout) Peace, Love And Understanding  (Curtis Singers)  (4:04)
11 Waiting For You  (Kenny G)  (2:43)
12 Trust In Me  (Joe Cocker)  (4:12)
13 Theme From The Bodyguard  (2:40)
14 I'm Every Woman  (Whitney Houston)  (10:37)
15 Queen Of The Night  (Whitney Houston)  (6:35)

Total album length: 75 minutes

KEVIN COSTNER
WHITNEY HOUSTON
THE BODYGUARD
ORIGINAL MOTION PICTURE SOUNDTRACK

# 1 Come On Over

| • Album sales: 22,000,000 | • Release date: November 1997 |

Country singer Shania Twain's third album, *Come On Over*, her second with husband and producer Mutt Lange, consolidated the twosome's reputation as a self-contained hit factory. All 16 cuts on the album were written by the husband-and-wife team – and the hits and awards were plentiful.

**Number One singles:**
None

**Grammy awards:** Best female country vocal performance – Man I Feel Like A Woman, You're Still The One; Best country song – Come On Over, You're Still The One

**Label:** US & UK: Mercury

**Recorded in:** N/A

**Personnel:**
Shania Twain
Brian White
Joe Chemay
Bruce Bouton
Larry Byrom
Stuart Duncan
Larry Franklin
Paul Franklin
Rob Hajacos
John Hobbs
Dann Huff
John Hughey
John Jarvis
Robert John 'Mutt Lange
Paul Leim
Carl Marsh
Brent Mason
Glenn Meadows
Joey Miskulin
Michael Omartian
Olle Romo
Eric Silver
Various other personnel

**Producer:**
Robert John 'Mutt' Lange

Sales were supported by an ambitious tour and four Grammys, including Best Female Country Vocal Performance for 'Man! I Feel Like a Woman!' and Best Country Song for 'Come On Over'. Another song from the album, 'You're Still the One', had won the same two awards at the previous year's awards ceremony.

The couple's pop sensibility was now clearly defined, dressing up country idioms in fashionable rock clothes. *Come On Over* went on to gain 22 platinum awards.

1  Man! I Feel Like A Woman! (3:53)
2  I'm Holdin' On To Love (To Save My Life) ( 3:30)
3  Love Gets Me Every Time (3:33)
4  Don't Be Stupid (You Know I Love You) (3:35)
5  From This Moment On  (4:43)
6  Come On Over (2:55)
7  When (3:39)
8  Whatever You Do! Don't! (4:04)
9  If You Wanna Touch Her, Ask! (4:04)
10 You're Still The One (3:34)
11 Honey, I'm Home (3:39)
12 That Don't Impress Me Much (3:38)
13 Black Eyes, Blue Tears (3:39)
14 I Won't Leave You Lonely (4:13)
15 Rock This Country! (4:23)
16 You've Got A Way (3:24)

Total album length: 60 minutes

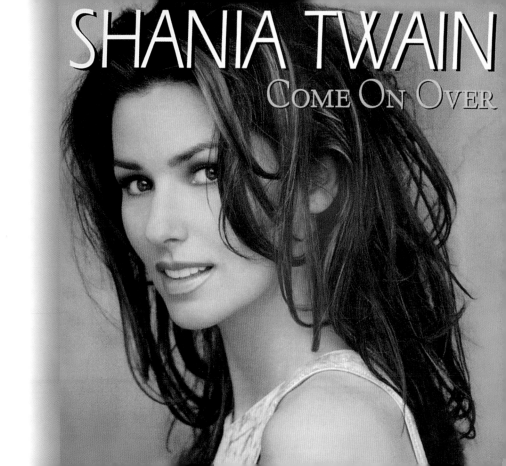

# Appendix: Facts and figures

**The 20 highest-ranking US artists (position on list given in brackets)**

1 Whitney Houston: *The Bodyguard* (2)
2 Hootie & The Blowfish: *Cracked Rear View* (4)
3 Garth Brooks: *No Fences* (5)
4 Santana: *Supernatural* (7)
5 Backstreet Boys: *Backstreet Boys* (8)
6 Britney Spears: *Baby One More Time* (10)
7 Metallica: *Metallica* (12)
8 Dixie Chicks: *Wide Open Spaces* (15)
9 Kenny G: *Breathless* (17)
10 Pearl Jam: *Ten* (18)
11 Matchbox 20: *Yourself Or Someone Like You* (19)
12 Boyz II Men: *II* (20)
13 Mariah Carey: *Music Box* (23)
14 TLC: *CrazySexyCool* (24)
15 Kid Rock: *Devil Without A Cause* (25)
16 Jewel: *Pieces Of You* (26)
17 Nirvana: *Nevermind* (29)
18 MC Hammer: *Please Hammer Don't Hurt 'Em* (30)
19 No Doubt: *Tragic Kingdom* (31)
20 Green Day: *Dookie* (33)

**The 20 highest-ranking UK or international artists**

1 Shania Twain (Canada): *Come On Over* (1)
2 Alanis Morissette (Canada): *Jagged Little Pill* (3)
3 Celine Dion (Canada): *Falling Into You* (13)
4 Eric Clapton (UK): *Unplugged* (27)
5 Spice Girls (UK): *Spice* (37)
6 U2 (Ireland): *Achtung Baby* (41)
7 Ace Of Base (Sweden): *The Sign* (43)
8 Sarah McLachlan (Canada): *Surfacing* (58)
9 Oasis (UK): *(What's The Story) Morning Glory* (62)
10 Savage Garden (Australia): *Savage Garden* (64)
11 Ricky Martin (Puerto Rica): *Ricky Martin* (67)
12 Bush (UK): *Sixteen Stone* (94)
13 Mana (Mexico): *Donde Jugaran Los Ninos?* (98)

**Live albums in the Top 100**

1 *Double Live*: Garth Brooks (06)
2 *Unplugged*: Eric Clapton (27)

## The 10 highest-ranking solo artists

1 Shania Twain: *Come On Over* (1)
2 Whitney Houston: *The Bodyguard* (2)
3 Alanis Morissette: *Jagged Little Pill* (3)
4 Garth Brooks: *No Fences* (5)
5 Britney Spears: *Baby One More Time* (10)
6 Celine Dion: *Falling Into You* (13)
7 Kenny G: *Breathless* (17)
8 Mariah Carey: *Music Box* (23)
9 Kid Rock: *Devil Without A Cause* (25)
10 Jewel: *Pieces Of You* (26)

## The 10 highest-ranking bands

1 Hootie & The Blowfish: *Cracked Rear View* (4)
2 Backstreet Boys: *Backstreet* (8)
3 Metallica: *Metallica* (12)
4 Dixie Chicks: *Wide Open Spaces* (15)
5 Pearl Jam: *Ten* (18)
6 Matchbox 20: *Yourself Or Someone Like You* (19)
7 Boyz II Men: *II* (20)
8 TLC: *CrazySexyCool* (24)
9 Nirvana: *Nevermind* (29)
10 No Doubt: *Tragic Kingdom* (31)

## Record labels with the most albums in the Top 100

1 Arista (14 albums)
2 Epic (13 albums)
3 Columbia (10 albums)
4 Capitol (9 albums)
5 Atlantic (8 albums)
6 Jive (5 albums)
7 La Face (5 albums)
8 Geffen (4 albums)
9 RCA (4 albums)
10 Virgin (4 albums)
11 Warners (4 albums)
12 550 Music (3 albums)
13 Interscope (3 albums)
14 Island (3 albums)
15 Mercury (3 albums)
16 Polygram (3 albums)

## Soundtrack albums in the Top 100

1 *The Bodyguard*: Whitney Houston (2)
2 *Forrest Gump*: Various Artists (16)
3 *Titanic*: Various Artists (21)
4 *The Lion King*: Various Artists (32)
5 *Waiting To Exhale*: Various Artists (80)
6 *Space Jam*: Various Artists (87)

**Artists with the most albums in the Top 100**
**(artists ranked by number of albums and aggregate score of album positions)**

1   **Garth Brooks:**
    *No Fences* (5)
    *Double Live* (6)
    *Ropin' The Wind* (9)
    *In Pieces* (54)
    *The Chase* (61)
    *Sevens* (73)
    *Fresh Horses* (88)

2   **Mariah Carey**
    *Music Box* (23)
    *Daydream* (28)
    *Mariah Carey* (40)

3   **Celine Dion**
    *Falling Into You* (13)
    *Let's Talk About Love* (22)
    *The Colour Of My Love* (66)

4   **Shania Twain**
    *Come On Over* (1)
    *The Woman In Me* (14)

5   **Backstreet Boys**
    *Backstreet Boys* (8)
    *Millennium* (11)

6   **Dixie Chicks**
    *Wide Open Spaces* (15)
    *Fly* (34)

7   **Boyz II Men**
    *II* (20)
    *ColeyHighHarmoney* (45)

8   **Kenny G**
    *Breathless* (17)
    *Miracles* (59)

9   **Pearl Jam**
    *Ten* (18)
    *Vs.* (76)

10  **Toni Braxton**
    *Secrets* (49)
    *Toni Braxton* (55)

11  **TLC**
    *CrazySexyCool* (24)
    *Fanmail* (84)

## Albums containing the most Number One singles

**1**  *Mariah Carey*: **Mariah Carey**
4 Number Ones: US: Vision Of Love; Love Takes Time; Some Day; I Don't Wanna Cry

**2**  *Spice:* **Spice Girls**
4 Number Ones: US & UK: Wannabe; UK: Say You'll Be There; 2 Become 1; Who Do You Think You Are

**3**  *Christina Aguilera*: **Christina Aguilera**
3 Number Ones: US & UK: Genie In A Bottle; US: What A Girl Wants; Come On Over Baby (All I Want Is You)

**4**  *Daydream*: **Mariah Carey**
3 Number Ones: US: Fantasy; One Sweet Day; Always Be My Baby

**5**  *Music Box*: **Mariah Carey**
3 Number Ones: US: Dreamlover; Hero; UK: Without You

**6**  *No Way Out*: **Puff Daddy**
2 Number Ones: US & UK: I'll Be Missing You; US: Can't Nobody Hold Me Down

**7**  *Baby One More Time*: **Britney Spears**
2 Number Ones: US & UK: Baby One More Time; UK: Born To Make You Happy

## Albums that have won the most Grammys

**1**  *Supernatural*: Santana (8 Grammys)
**2**  *Unplugged*: Eric Clapton (6 Grammys)
**3**  *The Miseducation Of Lauryn Hill*: Lauryn Hill (5 Grammys)
**4**  *Come On Over*: Shania Twain (4 Grammys)
**5**  *Jagged Little Pill*: Alanis Morissette (4 Grammys)
**6**  *Let's Talk About Love*: Celine Dion (4 Grammys)
**7**  *Titanic Soundtrack*: Various Artists (3 Grammys)
**8**  *Please Hammer Don't Hurt 'Em*: MC Hammer (3 Grammys)
**9**  *R*: R. Kelly (3 Grammys)
**10**  *Toni Braxton*: Toni Braxton (3 Grammys)
**11**  *Breathe*: Faith Hill (3 Grammys)
**12**  *Tuesday Night Music Club*: Sheryl Crow (3 Grammys)
**13**  *Luck Of The Draw*: Bonnie Raitt (3 Grammys)
**14**  *Space Jam*: Various Artists (3 Grammys)
**15**  *Cracked Rear View*: Hootie & The Blowfish (2 Grammys)
**16**  *Falling Into You*: Celine Dion (2 Grammys)
**17**  *Wide Open Spaces*: Dixie Chicks (2 Grammys)
**18**  *II*: Boyz II Men (2 Grammys)
**19**  *CrazySexyCool*: TLC (2 Grammys)
**20**  *The Lion King*: Various Artists (2 Grammys)
**21**  *Fly*: Dixie Chicks (2 Grammys)
**22**  *Mariah Carey*: Mariah Carey (2 Grammys)
**23**  *Secrets*: Toni Braxton (2 Grammys)
**24**  *Surfacing*: Sarah McLachlan (2 Grammys)
**25**  *The Score*: The Fugees (2 Grammys)
**26**  *Fanmail*: TLC (2 Grammys)
**27**  *2001*: Dr. Dre (2 Grammys)

# Index

'2 Become 1', 142
*12 Play*, 36–7
*2001*, 46–7

Ace Of Base, 128–9
*Achtung Baby*, 12, 134–5
'Achy Breaky Heart', 128
'Adia', 100
Adler, Steve, 78
Aguilera, Christina, 114–15, 219
albums
    with the most Grammys, 219
    with the most No. 1 singles, 219
    *see also* live albums
Alice In Chains, 146
'All By Myself', 190
*All Eyez On Me*, 112–13
'All I Really Want', 210
'All I Wanna Do', 86
Ament, Jeff, 180
'Am I The Only One
    (Who's Ever Felt This...)', 186
'Angel', 100
'Another Sad Love Song', 106
Armstrong, Billie Joe, 150
artists, highest-ranking
    most albums in the Top 100, 218
    solo artists, 217
    UK or International, 216
    US, 216
*August And Everything After*, 62–3
Austin, Dallas, 126

Babyface, 176
*Baby One More Time*, 196–7, 219

Backstreet Boys, 11–12, 218
    *Backstreet Boys*, 200–1
    *Millenium*, 194–5
Ballard, Glen, 210
bands, highest-ranking, 217
'Basket Case', 150
*Bat Out Of Hell II*, 52–3
'Because You Loved Me', 84, 190
'Before You Accuse Me', 162
*Big Willie Style*, 140–1
'Bills, Bills, Bills', 124
'Black Or White', 122
Blige, Mary J., 120
*Blood Sugar Sex Magik*, 80–1
*Blue*, 30–1
Blues Traveler, 24–5
*Bodyguard, The*, 10, 212–13
Bolton, Michael, 132–3
'Bomb', 28
Bono, 134
Bottrell, Bill, 122
Boyz II Men, 15, 218
    *Cooleyhighharmony*, 126–7
    *II*, 176–7
Braxton, Toni, 218
    *Secrets*, 118–19
    *Toni Braxton*, 106–7
'Break My Stride', 154
*Breathe*, 102–3
*Breathless*, 182–3
Brooks, Garth, 10, 218
    *Double Live*, 204–5
    *Fresh Horses*, 40–1
    *In Pieces*, 108–9
    *No Fences*, 206–7

    *Ropin' The Wind*, 198–9
    *Sevens*, 70–1
    *The Chase*, 94–5
'Brother John', 24
Bryson, Peabo, 182
'Bullet With Butterfly Wings', 138
Burnett, T-Bone, 62
Bush, 12, 28–9
'By The Time The Night Is Over', 182

'California Love', 112
'Can't Nobody Hold Me Down', 68
'Can You Feel The Love Tonight?', 152
Carey, Mariah, 15, 218
    *Daydream*, 160–1, 219
    *Mariah Carey*, 136–7, 219
    *Music Box*, 14, 170–1, 219
Cavallo, Rob, 150
'Change, The', 40
*Chase, The*, 94–5
*Christina Aguilera*, 114–15, 219
'Circle of Life', 152
Clapton, Eric, 10, 162–3
Cobain, Kurt, 158
*Colour Of My Love, The* ,84–5
Combs, Sean 'Puffy', 68
'Comedown', 28
*Come On Over*, 10, 214–15
'Come On Over', 214
'Come To My Window', 18
'Con Los Anos Que Me Quedan', 96
*Cooleyhighharmony*, 126–7
*Core*, 104–5
Counting Crows, 62–3
*Cracked Rear View*, 9, 208–9

Cranberries, The, 12, 90–1
*Crash*, 58–9
'Crash Into Me', 58
'(You Drive Me) Crazy', 196
*CrazySexyCool*, 168–9
Creed
    *Human Clay*, 146–7
    *My Own Prison*, 34–5
Crow, Sheryl, 11, 86–7
Cyrus, Billy Ray, 128–9

'Dance, The', 204
D'Angelo, 120
*Dangerous*, 122–3
Dave Matthews Band, The
    *Crash*, 58–9
    *Under The Table And Dreaming*,
    26–7
*Daydream*, 160–1
'Dead And Bloated', 104
DeLeo, Dean, 104
Destiny's Child, 124–5
*Devil Without A Cause*, 166–7
Dion, Celine, 116, 218
    *Colour Of My Love, The*, 84–5
    *Falling Into You*, 190–1
    *Let's Talk About Love*, 172–3
Dixie Chicks, 218
    *Fly*, 148–9
    *Wide Open Spaces*, 10, 186–7
DJ Lethal, 72
DJ Premier, 72
*Donde Jugaran Los Ninos*, 20–1
'Don't Look Back In Anger', 92
'Don't Speak', 154
'Don't Turn Around', 130
*Dookie*, 150–1
'Doo Wop (That Thing)', 120
*Double Live*, 204–5
Dr. Dre, 46–7

'Dreamlover', 170
Dupri, Jermaine, 44
Duritz, Adam, 62
Durst, Fred, 72
Dylan, Bob, 132

Eagles, The, 66–7
Elliott, Missy, 124
Eminem, 46
'End Of The Night', 182
'End Of The Road', 15
Eno, Brian, 134
Enrique, Luis, 96
Erwin, Emily, 186
Estefan, Gloria, 96–7
Etheridge, Melissa, 18–19
'Everything Zen', 28
'Exhale', 56

facts and figures, 6–7
*Falling Into You*, 190–1
*Fanmail*, 48–9
'Fantasy', 160
'Fever, The', 40
Fher, 20
*Fly*, 148–9
'Fly, The', 134
'Forever In Love', 182
'Forgiven', 210
*Forrest Gump*, 184–5
Foster, David, 118
*Four*, 24–5
*Fresh Horses*, 40–1
'Friends In Low Places', 204, 206
Fugees, The, 14, 14–15, 74–5

Gallagher, Noel and Liam, 92
'Genie In A Bottle', 114
'Get Down (You're The One For Me)', 200
'Get Over It', 66

'Give It Away', 80
'Give It Up Or Let Me Go', 186
'Glycerine', 28
'Go III', 76
'Goodbye Earl', 148
Gossard, Stone, 180
Grammy awards, 219
Green Day, 150–1
'Greensleeves', 98
Guns N' Roses, 78–9

Hammer, MC *see* MC Hammer
'Happy Nation', 130
Harrison, Jerry, 110
'Have Yourself A Merry Little Christmas',
    98
'Have You Seen Her', 156
'Heartland', 16
*Hell Freezes Over*, 66–7
Henley, Don, 66
'Hero', 170
Hetfield, James, 13
Hill, Faith, 102–3
Hill, Lauryn, 15, 120–1
'Hold My Hand', 208
'Home Alone', 116
Hootie & The Blowfish, 9, 208–9
Horner, James, 174
Houston, Whitney, 10, 212–13
*Human Clay*, 146–7
'Hypnotize', 144

'I Believe I Can Fly', 42, 116
'Ice Ice Baby', 76
'I Cross My Heart', 16
'I'd Do Anything For Love (But I Won't Do
    That)', 52
'I Don't Wanna Cry', 136
'If I Was Your Girlfriend', 168
*II*, 176–7

'I'll Be Missing You', 68
'I'm Every Woman', 212
'I'm The Only One', 18
'I'm Your Angel', 116
'In Lonesome Dove', 198
*In Pieces,* 108–9
'It's All Coming Back To Me Now', 190
'I Used To Love Him', 120
'I Want It That Way', 194
'I Want You', 88
'I Want You Back', 60
'I Will Always Love You', 212
'I Will Get There', 15
'I Will Never Be The Same', 18

Jackson, Janet, 50–1
Jackson, Michael, 122–3
*Jagged Little Pill,* 11, 210–11
Jam, Jimmy, 50, 176
*Janet,* 50–1
Jenkins, Rodney, 124
Jenkins, Stephan, 32
Jennings, Will, 174
Jewel, 164–5
Joel, Bill, 198
'Joy Of Life, The', 182
'Just The Two Of Us', 140

Kanal, Tony, 154
Kelly, R., 14
    *12 Play,* 36–7
    *R,* 116–17
Kenny G, 132, 218
    *Breathless,* 182–3
    *Miracles: The Holiday Album,* 98–9
Khan, Chaka, 56
'Killing Me Softly', 14
Knowles, Beyoncé, 124
Kriesel, Greg, 22
Kurzweg, John Philip, 146

LaBelle, Patti, 132
Lange, 'Mutt', 188, 214
Langer, Clive, 28
Lanois, Daniel, 134
'Last Dance', 100
'Layla', 162
'Learn To Be Still', 66
Lethal, DJ, 72
'Let Her Cry', 208
'Let It Flow', 118
'Let's Make Love', 102
*Let's Talk About Love,* 172–3
Lewis, Terry, 50, 176
*Life After Death,* 144–5
'Lightning Crashes', 110
Lillywhite, Steve, 58, 134
Limp Bizkit, 72–3
*Lion King, The,* 152–3
'Little Things', 28
Live, 110–11
live albums
    *Double Live,* 204–5
    *Unplugged,* 10, 162–3
'Living In Danger', 130
'Livin' La Vida Loca', 82
'Longview', 150
Lopes, Lisa 'Left Eye', 140, 168
'Love Is A Wonderful Thing', 132
'Love Takes Time', 136
*Luck Of The Draw,* 54–5
Lundin, Kristian, 60

Mack, Bill, 30
McLagan, Ian, 18
Maines, Lloyd, 148
Maines, Natalie, 186
'Mama', 142
Mana, 20–1
'Man! I Feel Like A Woman', 214
Marchand, Pierre, 100

*Mariah Carey,* 136–7, 219
'Maria Maria', 202
Marquez, Juanito, 96
Martin, Max, 60, 194, 196
Matchbox, 20, 178–9
MC Hammer, 13–14, 156–7
Meat Loaf, 10, 52–3
*Mellon Collie And The Infinite Sadness,* 138–9
Metallica, 13, 192–3
*Millenium,* 194–5
*Miracles: The Holiday Album,* 98–9
*Miseducation of Lauryn Hill, The,* 15, 120–1
*Mi Tierra,* 96–7
'Mo Money Mo Problems', 144
Morissette, Alanis, 10–11, 210–11
MP3 format, 8–9
'Mr Blue', 206
'Mr Jones', 62
Murray, Keith, 116
*Music Box,* 14, 170–1, 219
'My Funny Valentine', 56
'My Heart Will Go On', 172, 174
*My Own Prison,* 34–5
*My Way,* 44–5
'My Way', 44

*Nevermind,* 13, 158–9
Neville, Aaron, 182
'New Way To Fly', 206
'Nice & Slow', 44
Nirvana, 13, 158–9
No Doubt, 154–5
*No Fences,* 206–7
*No Need To Argue,* 12, 90–1
'Nookie', 72
'Nothing Even Matters', 120
Notorious B.I.G., The 14
    *Life After Death,* 144–5

*No Way Out*, 68–9, 219
\*N Sync 12, 60–1
*\*N Sync*, 60–1

Oasis, 12, 92–3
O'Brien, Brendan, 38
'Ode To My Family', 90
Offspring, 22–3
'One', 134
'One Part Be My Lover', 54
'One Sweet Day', 160
O'Riordan, Dolores, 90

Parton, Dolly, 212
'Peace, Love and Understanding', 212
Pearl Jam, 218
  *Ten*, 12–13, 180–1
  *Vs.*, 64–5
Pearlman, Lou, 60
*Pieces Of You*, 164–5
pirates, CD, 8
*Please Hammer, Don't Hurt 'Em*,
  14, 156–7
'Plush', 104
'Polly', 158
Pop, Denniz, 60
'Power Of Love, The', 84
'Pray', 156
Premier, DJ, 72
Puff Daddy & The Family, 68–9, 219
*Pure Country*, 16–17
*Purple*, 38–9

*R.*, 116–17
Raitt, Bonnie, 11, 54–5
'Ready Or Not', 74
record labels, 217
Red Hot Chilli Peppers, 80–1
Ricky Martin, 82–3
Riley, Terry, 122

Rimes, LeAnn, 30–1
'River Deep, Mountain High', 190
'River, The', 198
Rock, Bob, 192
Rock, Kid, 166–7
'Rodeo, The', 198
*Ropin' The Wind*, 198–9
Rossdale, Gavin, 28
Rubin, Rick, 80
Rundgren, Todd, 52
'Run To You', 212

Saint-Germain, Ron, 34
Santana, 9–10, 202–3
Santana, Carlos, 120, 202
Savage Garden, 88–9
*Savage Garden*, 88–9
'Say My Name', 124
'Say You'll Be There', 142
*Score, The*, 14, 14–15, 74–5
*Secrets*, 118–19
*Secret Samhadi*, 110
Seidel, Martie, 186
'Semi-Charmed Life', 32
*Sevens*, 70–1
'Seven Whole Days', 106
'Sex Me, Pts 1-2', 36
'Sex Type Thing', 104
Shakur, Tupac, 14, 112
'Shameless', 204
Sheehan, Bobby, 24
'She's All I Ever Had', 82
'She's Every Woman', 40
'Show Me The Meaning Of Being Lonely',
  194
'Signe', 162
*Significant Other*, 72–3
*Sign, The*, 130–1
*Sixteen Stone*, 28–9
Slovak, Hillel, 80

Smalls, Biggie, 144
*Smash*, 22–3
Smashing Pumpkins, 138–9
Smith, Will, 14–15, 140–1
'Smooth', 202
'Someday', 136
*Some Gave All*, 128–9
'Something In The Way', 158
'Sometimes', 196
Sorum, Matt, 78
Soundgarden, 146
soundtracks
  *The Bodyguard*, 10, 212–13
  *Forrest Gump*, 184–5
  *The Lion King*, 152–3
  *Space Jam*, 42–3
  *Titanic*, 174–5
  *Waiting To Exhale*, 56–7
*Space Jam*, 42–3
Spears, Britney, 12
  *Baby One More Time*, 196–7, 219
*Spice*, 142–3, 219
Spice Girls, The, 12, 142–3, 219
Stapp, Scott, 34, 146
Stefani, Gwen, 154
Steinman, Jim, 52, 190
Stiger, Curtis, 212
'Still D R E', 46
Stone Temple Pilots
  *Core*, 104–5
  *Purple*, 38–9
Strait, George, 16–17
Street, Stephen, 90
'Strong Enough', 86
'Super Freak', 156
*Supernatural*, 9–10, 202–3
*Surfacing*, 100–1
Swedlen, Bruce, 122
'Tears In Heaven', 162
*Ten*, 12–13, 180–1

'That's The Way Love Goes', 50
'That Summer', 204
'Think Twice', 84
Third Eye Blind, 32–3
*Third Eye Blind*, 32–3
Thomas, Rozonda, 168
*Throwing Copper*, 110–11
'Thunder Rolls, The', 204
Timberlake, Justin, 12
*Time, Love & Tenderness*, 132–3
*Titanic,* 174–5
TLC, 218
   *CrazySexyCool*, 168–9
   *Fanmail*, 48–9
*Toni Braxton,* 106–7
*To The Extreme*, 76–7
'To Zion', 120
'Tradicion', 96
*Tragic Kingdom*, 154–5
Tremonti, Mark, 146
'Tripping Billies', 58
*Tuesday Night Music Club,* 86–7
Tupac, 112–13
Twain, Shania, 8, 218
   *Come On Over,* 10, 214–15
   *The Woman In Me,* 188–9

U2, 12, 134–5
'U Can't Touch This', 156
'Unanswered Prayers', 204
'Un-Break My Heart', 118

'Under The Bridge', 80
*Under The Table And Dreaming*, 26–7
United Kingdom, album sales, 9
United States, album sales, 9
*Unplugged*, 10, 162–3
'Unpretty', 48
*Use Your Illusion I & II,* 78–9
Usher, 44–5

Valentine, Eric, 32
Vanilla Ice, 76–7
Vedder, Eddie, 64, 180
Vig, Butch, 158
'Vision Of Love', 136
*Vs.,* 64–5

Wachtel, Wendy, 18
*Waiting To Exhale,* 56–7
'Wannabe', 142
Warren, Diane, 132
Was, Don, 54
'Waterfalls', 168
Watkins, Tionne, 168
Weiland, Scott, 104
'We Shall Be Free', 94
*(What's The Story) Morning Glory?,* 92–3
'What Would You Say?', 26
'When Did You Stop Loving Me', 16
'When I Come Around', 150
'When I Fall In Love', 84
'When I Need You', 172

'Where Will The Children Play?', 20
'White Discussion', 110
'Who Do You Think You Are', 142
'Who's Bed Have Your Boots Been
   Under?', 188
'Who Will Save Your Soul', 164
*Wide Open Spaces*, 10, 186–7
Wiggins, Dwayne, 124
Wilder, Matthew, 152
'Wild Horses', 206
Wilson, Thom, 22
Winstanley, Alan, 28
*Woman In Me, The,* 188–9
'Wonderwall', 92
Wood, Andrew, 180
Wright, Donna, 12
*Writing's On The Wall, The,* 124–5

*Yes I Am,* 18–19
'(You Drive Me) Crazy', 196
'You Make Me Wanna', 44
'You Mean The World To Me', 106
'Young And Proud', 130
'Your Body's Callin', 36
'You're Makin' Me High', 118
'You're Still The One', 214
*Yourself Or Someone Like You,* 178–9
'You Win My Love', 188

'Zombie', 90